HOW TO COOK
Indian Curry
in the Slow Cooker

The culinary tradition that suits the slow cooker perfectly

Catherine Atkinson

foulsham
LONDON • NEW YORK • TORONTO • SYDNEY

foulsham

Capital Point, 33 Bath Road, Slough, Berkshire, SL1 3UF,
England

Foulsham books can be found in all good bookshops and direct from
www.foulsham.com

ISBN: 978-0-572-03749-9

Copyright © 2012 W. Foulsham & Co. Ltd

Cover photographs: top © Crock-Pot; bottom left © Fresh Food Images;
bottom right by Terry Pastor

A CIP record for this book is available from the British Library

You may also be interested in:
How to cook comfort food on a tight budget
How to cook complete meals in your halogen cooker

Printed in Great Britain by Cox & Wyman, Reading

contents

introduction

When I was young, we all looked forward to 'curry night' when my mother would serve a chicken or meat casserole cooked with a handful of sultanas – or if we were lucky, a tin of pineapple – sprinkled on after cooking with a teaspoon or two of curry powder. It was a far cry from authentic Indian cooking. Over the last 20 years or so, our love of Indian food has grown and so has our knowledge – we are now aware of the huge variety and subtlety that this cuisine has to offer. Many of us regularly dine in Indian restaurants and buy ready-prepared curries. At the end of a busy day you are likely to feel tired, hungry and looking forward to sitting down and enjoying a meal. Rather than dashing out for a takeaway or settling for a chilled meal from a packet, wouldn't it be great to serve a delicious home-cooked Indian curry from your slow cooker, ready to serve with rice or accompany with warm breads? This book is packed with a whole range of curry and spicy dishes. Some use curry pastes to keep preparation to an absolute minimum and some have a combination of fresh spices that you blend yourself; at last, you can bring the flavour of your local curry restaurant to your home. The basic principle behind the slow cooker is that it cooks food slowly at a constant temperature. This is the way that Indian food has been made for centuries and one of the greatest advantages of making curries in the slow cooker is that it develops and enhances the flavour of food; it allows spices to release all their essential oils, giving a real depth and intensity to the finished dish. While vegetables retain their texture, it makes even the toughest meat meltingly tender, making long marinating unnecessary.

Slow cookers are also environmentally friendly; their low wattage consumes about the same amount of electricity as a light bulb. They can save up to five times the energy of stove-top and conventional oven cooking, making them ideal for those on a budget. The essentials of slow cooking are incredibly simple, but do have a look at pages 15–20 before you begin.

Our Menu

Browse Our Menu

Browse through our menu to take your pick of the superb selection on offer, from the mildest curries to those with a real kick.

Our Menu

Chicken and duck

Chicken korma
Coconut, almonds and cream are the keynotes of a rich, mildly spiced sauce that bathes the chicken. *p22*

Tandoori chicken
Marinating in a spiced yoghurt mixture with lime and paprika creates meltingly tender chicken portions. *p24*

Chicken with spinach and lentils
Coriander-spiced chicken thighs are gently simmered with spinach and lentils until the sauce is creamy, then served on a bed of rice. *p26*

Saffron-scented chicken
Beneath the toasted almonds, the unmistakeable golden colour and aroma of saffron emerges from the mildly spiced creamy sauce with a touch of honey. *p28*

Chicken with cashew sauce
Rich yet delicately flavoured, this Mughlai is based on a curry paste with spices, onions, garlic and cashews. *p30*

Northern chicken curry
Redolent with the robust flavours of the Punjab – onions, tomatoes, garlic, ginger and garam masala infuse this. *p32*

Chicken mangalore
Chillies and coconut are the typical flavours in this southern-region dish, spiced with a hint of cinnamon, cloves, ginger and coriander. *p34*

Chicken with red lentils
A dhanzak curry, medium spiced with a sweet-sour touch of sugar and vinegar, with chunks of chicken and potato in a thick sauce of soft lentils. *p36*

Chicken biryani
The crunch of cashews enlivens this lightly spiced rice dish with chicken, onion, cauliflower and peas stirred through perfectly cooked rice. *p38*

Chicken jalfrezi
Meaning 'dry fry', this hottish curry of chicken, peppers, tomatoes and a collection of exotic spices has just enough sauce to coat the tender chicken thighs. *p40*

Butter chicken
A Punjabi dish from the Moghul empire, the buttery smooth sauce thickened with cashew nuts makes murgh makhani a rich and satisfying dish. *p42*

Spiced duck
Cooked with jaggery – unrefined sugar from boiled date-palm sap – to give a unique flavour to tender duck breasts with spices, onions and ginger. *p44*

Coconut duck curry
A superb curry from Kerala with a sauce made with both coconut milk and freshly grated coconut for an intensely creamy finish. *p46*

Royal duck biryani
Created for serving to royalty, this dish combines rice, duck and vegetables and is spiced with cardamom and fragrant with saffron. *p48*

Lamb

Lamb korma
Ground almonds contribute to the creamy sauce, with garam masala and thick yoghurt for the perfect finish. *p52*

Indian lamb with spiced lentils
Green lentils, fragrant with garlic, ginger and spices, surround cubes of tender lean lamb in this dish. *p54*

Aromatic lamb
A complete dish of chunks of lamb and potatoes spiced with cinnamon, cloves and ginger. *p56*

Lamb dopiaza
Onions are the key flavour here, perfectly complementing the multi-spiced lamb softened with thick yoghurt. *p58*

Rogan josh
Red chillies, paprika and tomatoes give this dish the red of its name, while the spice selection gives the real kick. *p60*

Lamb parsi
Marinating in yoghurt moistens and tenderises the lamb before simmering it gently with potatoes and onions. *p62*

Spicy lamb with sweet potatoes
So soft, the sweet potatoes melt on your tongue with a sweetness that perfectly complements the tender lamb. *p64*

Spiced lamb in almond sauce
A fragrant blend of cardamom and cinnamon and a surprising fierce kick from the addition of green chillies. *p66*

Madras lamb curry
A fairly hot and fiery dish made with Madras curry paste – a blend of ground coriander, cumin, chilli, turmeric and garlic. Yoghurt gives the sauce a smooth finish. *p68*

Slow-cooked leg of lamb
Infused with spices, garlic and ginger, then slow-roasted until the lamb almost falls from the bone. *p70*

Kashmir lamb curry
Beautifully tender slow-cooked lamb shanks in a very mild, yet wonderfully fragrant sauce. Fennel gives an undertone of aniseed. *p72*

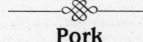

Pork

Hot and sour pork curry
Classic Goan cooking, vinegar gives a slight sharpness that contrasts with the richness of the meat – here, pieces of belly pork. *p76*

Goan pork curry
Tamarind intensifies the flavour of balsamic vinegar but is balanced by a good spoonful of jaggery, an unrefined sugar, making a wonderful sauce for strips of pork. *p78*

Pork korma with spinach
A mild curry with tasty lean pork mince, new potatoes and baby spinach leaves, cooked in a subtly-spiced almond and yoghurt sauce. *p80*

Beef

Beef biryani
Meltingly tender beef with ginger, cinnamon, cardamom, chilli, caraway and garam masala all cooked in a yoghurt sauce. *p84*

Bangladeshi beef curry
A thick spicy curry with chunks of beef so tender they can be cut with a spoon. The meat is moistened with just enough of the delicious sauce to coat the pieces. *p86*

Beef keema
A mellow curry made with minced beef and subtly spiced with a mild curry paste, extra ginger and optional green chilli, all in a tomato sauce. *p88*

Madras beef curry
A popular Indian dish, here individual spices are ground to a paste to give this curry an authentic flavour. *p90*

Beef pathia
Lean braising steak features in this medium-hot curry with its distinctive sweet and sour taste provided by a combination of tamarind and tomatoes. *p92*

Beef in spiced yoghurt
Only a few ingredients are used in this fuss-free 'dum gosht': lean beef, garlic, onions, paprika, ginger and cayenne pepper cooked in beef stock and yoghurt. *p94*

Beef pasanda
A spicy beef curry with a thick sauce made from almonds and cashew nuts, coconut, milk and cream.
A dash of lemon juice cuts through the richness. *p96*

Royal beef with almond sauce
A beef korma with a well-flavoured, yet mild rich sauce, inspired centuries ago and served to Indian royals. *p98*

Beef bhuna
Beef added to a rich spicy blend, gently cooking in its own juices with little liquid added. This results in superbly flavoured meat, to make a memorable meal. *p100*

Fish and seafood

Keralan fish curry
The combination of dried red chillies and coconut milk is frequently used in South Indian cooking. *p102*

Creamy coconut salmon
Here, salmon is cooked in a rich sauce made from a fragrant blend of spices, garlic and chilli. Coconut milk mellows the sauce and gives it a thick texture. *p104*

Mackerel curry with coconut
This traditional dish has the contrasting taste of sweet and creamy coconut and tangy tamarind that enhances the strong flavour of the mackerel. *p106*

Mangalorean fish curry
Chunks of firm white fish are cooked in a rich sauce spiced with cumin, coriander, chilli, turmeric, tamarind and mustard seeds. *p108*

Goan prawn curry
Made with large plump pink prawns, this colourful curry is a real winner. Warmly spiced and finished with a generous amount of fresh coriander. *p110*

Coconut jinga
A citrus, ginger and spice sauce is gently cooked to allow all the flavours to develop and mingle, then prawns added towards the end of cooking. *p112*

Kerala prawn curry
The signature notes of this dish are tamarind, ginger, chilli, garlic and coconut. Together they give the sauce a unique and distinctive taste. *p114*

King prawn and spinach balti
An easy curry using balti paste and large juicy prawns. Spinach and coriander provide plenty of colour and flavour and hot red chilli gives the dish a spicy punch. *p116*

Vegetable and vegetarian

Vegetable kashmiri
Potatoes, cauliflower and okra cooked in an aromatic yoghurt sauce and topped with a generous amount of toasted flaked almonds to add protein. *p120*

Potato and chick pea curry
Chunks of potatoes and chickpeas soak up all the flavours of garlic, ginger, cumin, coriander, cardamom and green chilli as they slowly cook until tender. *p122*

Vegetable curry
Loads of flavour: aubergine, red pepper, carrot, potato and broccoli all cooked in a lightly spiced sauce with tomatoes and the sweet taste of creamy coconut. *p124*

Chick pea curry
Blissfully simple, this is a homely curry using canned chickpeas and fresh ripe tomatoes in a sweet and tart pomegranate molasses, ginger and spice sauce. *p126*

Aubergine and lentil madras

Lentils and aubergines are a winning combination and a few soya beans add freshness and colour. *p128*

Eggs in mughlai sauce

An aromatic and creamy sauce with ginger, cumin, coriander and garam masala. Lemon juice adds sharpness and cayenne pepper a touch of heat. *p130*

Cauliflower and coconut dhal

Cauliflower, lentils and peas are a great mix for a curry. Coconut milk brings all the ingredients together. *p132*

Indian potatoes and okra

Potatoes and okra absorb the aroma of whole black mustard seeds and a range of ground spices as they cook. *p134*

Paneer korma

Cubes of paneer – a simple fresh cheese, similar to cottage cheese, but smooth – either home-made or bought, are added to a creamily spiced tomato sauce. *p136*

Vegetables with jaipuri spices

A subtly spiced curry; potatoes, carrots, green beans and fresh tomatoes make a colourful mixture. *p138*

Vegetable vindaloo

A colourful combination of chickpeas and vegetables are given a fiery kick with vindaloo curry paste. *p140*

Side dishes and accompaniments

Cooking rice

How to cook your rice so the grains remain separate but fluffy and delicious. *p142*

Mushroom pilau
The delicious juices from the mushrooms soak into the rice as this dish cooks. *p144*

Bombay potatoes
Here potatoes are cooked with turmeric, green chilli, coriander and cumin to make a fantastic side dish. *p146*

Mushroom bhaji
Classic Indian-style mushrooms with pungent spices, cooked in their own juices until tender. *p148*

Makhani dhal
Dhal is one of the staples of Indian cooking this version is a classic from the Punjab; buttery black lentils with onions, garlic, chillies and fresh ginger. *p150*

Tarka dhal
Red lentils cooked with tomatoes and flavoured with ginger, chilli and fresh coriander. 'Tarka', a mixture of spicy seeds, chilli and garlic, gives the dish zing. *p152*

Potato and cauliflower curry
Known as 'gobi aloo', potatoes and cauliflower are cooked with a wide range of spices in just a little stock. *p154*

Sweet mango chutney
A classic chutney with the rich vivid colour and fruity flavour of mangoes. Subtly spiced with ginger and crushed dried red chillies. *p156*

Cucumber and coriander raita
A cooling combination of cucumber and thick yoghurt scattered with fresh coriander to soften the bite of the hottest curries. *p158*

your slow cooker

For those who are new to slow cooking, here are some simple basics to get you started.

choosing a slow cooker

Slow cookers come in a wide variety of sizes, shapes, colours and prices and these factors need to be considered before you decide which one is right for you.

Appearance is the first thing you'll notice; you'll find contemporary stainless steel, rich-coloured and pristine-looking white models, as well as the rustic-looking cream and brown versions. There are round or oval ones, and the heat-resistant lid may be ceramic or toughened glass. The latter allows you to monitor the food without lifting the lid and losing precious heat.

The size of slow cookers ranges from a tiny 600 ml/1 pint/2½ cup cooking pot to a massive 6.5 litre/11½ pint/27 cup one, so choose a size that suits your needs. These recipes mainly serve four, so a 4 litre/7 pint/16 cup size is about right.

using and caring for your slow cooker

Because slow cooker models vary, make sure you read the manufacturer's instructions before using yours for the first time. Some slow cookers need to be preheated before you start cooking; others advise against heating it when empty. Before using for the first time, wash the inner ceramic cooking pot in hot soapy water, rinse and dry. You may notice a slight odour as the slow cooker heats up; this is caused by the burning off of manufacturing residues and should disappear after the first few uses. Don't worry if the ceramic glaze becomes slightly crazed; this is perfectly normal.

You'll notice that many of the recipes advise using very hot, not boiling, water and stock when adding it straight to the cooking pot. Never pour boiling water into the cold cooking pot (you can do so when it is already warm or hot, or when there are other ingredients covering the base), or plunge it into cold water immediately after use as this could crack it. Remember that it is an electrical appliance, so the outer casing should be wiped clean and never immersed in or filled with water.

When following a recipe, bear in mind that every model is slightly different and, even when using the same settings, some will cook much faster than others. For this reason a range of cooking times is given on most recipes; check after the shorter time given, as this will usually be sufficient, but the food won't spoil for the extra time. Some small models cook quite quickly on High, so you may prefer to use the Low setting. After trying a few recipes, you will know whether your slow cooker is faster or slower and be able to adjust the recipe cooking times accordingly.

safety

The slow cooker is a very safe appliance, but commonsense precautions should be followed. Although it cooks at a low temperature, the outer casing, lid and food inside may get extremely hot, so you should always use oven gloves when removing the ceramic cooking pot. Stand the slow cooker on a heat-resistant surface when in use, away from the edge where it might accidentally get knocked off, and make sure that the mains lead is tucked safely behind it. Take extra care that it's out of reach if you have young children or inquisitive pets.

Slow cookers cook food at a relatively low heat – around 90°C/194°F on the Low setting to about 150°C/300°F on the High setting. Any bacteria present in food is destroyed at 74°C/165°F, so as long as it's cooked for the correct time the temperature of the slow cooker will ensure that the food is safe to eat. You should take care, however, not to reduce the cooking temperature:

- Unless a recipe tells you to stir a dish part way through cooking, it should be left undisturbed and you should avoid lifting the lid. If you do need to lift the lid during cooking other than when specified, add an extra 10–15 minutes cooking time to make up for the heat loss.
- Ideally ingredients should be at room temperature when you start to cook; increase the cooking time if you use frozen vegetables. Never add frozen or part-frozen meat to the slow cooker.
- Avoid placing the slow cooker near a draught.
- Always check that meat is thoroughly cooked, particularly poultry and pork, preferably using a meat thermometer.

cooking times

The cooking temperatures and settings vary on different models, but most have four settings: Off, Low, High and Auto. Some also have a Medium setting. At the lowest temperature the food will barely simmer; at the highest it will boil very gently. When set to Auto, the cooking temperature will build up to High, then remain at this temperature for an hour or so before automatically switching to Low. This setting is useful if you are using frozen vegetables.

Food should be monitored when using the High setting as some liquid will evaporate. Some flexibility can be introduced to the total cooking time by adjusting the temperature settings. As a rough guide, the cooking time on Low is about double that of High.

Low	Auto or Medium	High
2–4	1½–2½	1–2
6–8	4–6	3–4
8–10	6–8	5–6

If at the end of the cooking time the food is not quite ready, replace the lid and switch the slow cooker to High. Once ready, many dishes (but not rice or fish) can be kept hot for an hour or more without any risk of spoiling, by switching to Low.

If you are planning to go out for the day and your chosen recipe does not take as many hours to cook as you will be away, you can use a time-delay plug so that the start of cooking is delayed by several hours. If you are going to delay the start of cooking, it's important that all the ingredients – including stock – are cold (preferably chilled) when added to the ceramic cooking pot. Never use a time-delay plug when cooking chicken or when the kitchen will be warm, e.g. on a sunny day or if the central heating will be on before cooking commences.

Modern slow cookers tend to cook at a slightly higher temperature than older ones, so if you have a newer model, check whether the food is ready at the minimum suggested cooking time.

tips for slow cooking curries

- Any of your usual curry recipes can be cooked in the slow cooker but remember that liquid doesn't evaporate as much as it does when cooking conventionally, so cut down the liquid content by 20–30 per cent. You can always add extra liquid at the end if necessary, to thin the sauce.

- Should there be too much liquid at the end of cooking, strain it into a saucepan and boil rapidly for several minutes until it is reduced to the quantity and consistency you require. Alternatively, you can thicken it with a little cornflour (cornstarch) blended with cold water, or a little extra creamed coconut, if appropriate.

- Many traditional Indian curry recipes include yoghurt. Although this would typically be plain yoghurt, thick plain or Greek-style yoghurts have been suggested here as ordinary plain yoghurt may separate after very long low-temperature cooking. For the same reason, some recipes have the addition of a tiny amount of cornflour, which will prevent the sauce from separating. Avoid using low-fat or reduced-fat yoghurts in the slow cooker; if you want to reduce the fat content of a dish, substitute stock for some of the yoghurt.

- Some of the recipes here call for 'ghee'; this is clarified butter that has been cooked so that its natural sugars caramelise a little, giving it a slightly nutty flavour. Unlike ordinary butter, it can withstand high temperature. Unsalted (sweet) butter can be substituted, but it is better if you clarify your own butter: gently melt unsalted butter until it separates into three layers. Skim off the white froth that floats to the top, then carefully tip the golden liquid in the middle into a container. Discard the milk solids at the bottom. Cool and store in the fridge – it will keep for several weeks.

- During cooking, steam condenses on the lid of the slow cooker, then trickles back into the pot, helping to retain heat and reduce strong cooking smells. Make sure that the lid is placed centrally on the cooking pot.

- Allow a 5 cm/2 in distance between the food and top of a ceramic cooking pot. While all the recipes in the book take this into account, bear it in mind if you decide to double the ingredients to make a larger amount.

- Onions and root vegetables, such as carrots, take longer to cook than meat as the liquid simmers rather than boils. Cut into smallish, even-sized chunks. For many dishes, it is best to fry onions before adding them as the flavour is different from when they are slow cooked from raw.

- It is preferable to thaw frozen vegetables before adding but it isn't essential. If time allows, spread them out on kitchen paper (paper towels) at room temperature to thaw.

- Ordinary long-grain rice doesn't cook well in the slow cooker, but easy-cook (converted rice) or 'parboiled' rice, will cook to perfection. It has been steamed under pressure, ensuring the grains remain separate.

- Fresh herbs cooked for a long time will lose their colour and pungency. Use dried herbs at the start of cooking and add fresh ones at the end. Many Indian recipes use fresh coriander (cilantro). You can substitute parsley, if you prefer.

- Some recipes use curry powders or pastes. There are many varieties and they vary in flavour, heat and spiciness.

Type	Main flavourings	Heat
Korma	Coconut and coriander	Mild
Tikka masala	Tomato and coconut	Medium
Balti	Tomato and coriander	Medium
Bhuna	Tomato and tamarind	Medium
Biryani	Coriander and cumin	Medium
Dhanzak	Tomato and cumin	Medium
Jalfrezi	Sweet pepper and coconut	Medium
Garam masala	Cinnamon and ginger	Hot
Madras	Cumin and chilli	Hot

notes on the recipes

- Do not mix metric, imperial and American measures. Follow one set only. American terms are given in brackets.

- All spoon measurements are level: 1 tsp = 5 ml; 1 tbsp = 15 ml.

- Always wash, peel, core, deseed etc. fresh foods before use. Ensure that all produce is as fresh as possible and that it is in good condition.

- If you want to save preparation time, use ready-prepared ingredients such as frozen diced onions and shallots, bottled or frozen grated ginger and garlic and chilli purées (pastes). The quantities needed are given as an alternative to their fresh counterpart in the recipes.

- Seasoning is very much a matter of personal taste. Sample the food before serving and adjust to suit your own palate.

- There is a wide range of chillies available. In general, the large, fat ones are milder than the thin ones. Most of the heat is in the seeds and white pith; these can be removed or left in, as you prefer.

- All cooking times are approximate and are intended as a guide only. Get to know your slow cooker; you will soon know if it cooks a little faster or slower than the times given.

- Can and packet sizes depend on the particular brand.

chicken and duck

Chicken makes simply great curries – the meat just soaks up all the fragrant spices. For succulence, flavour and versatility, it's an unbeatable combination. Plus, using the slow cooker allows the whole dish to become flavoursome and succulent. Some of the most popular Indian dishes include korma, tandoori and butter chicken. The slow cooker makes moist and flavoursome chicken curries whichever cut you choose: breast, quarters, thighs or drumsticks.

Buy poultry from a reliable source and refrigerate as soon as possible after purchase. If you can't cook it within a day or two, poultry will keep for up to three months in the freezer; defrost overnight in the refrigerator and always check that it is thawed before adding to the slow cooker. You should also make sure that larger pieces, such as portions and thighs, are thoroughly cooked before serving by piercing them at the thickest point; the juices should run clear and not at all pink.

You'll also find some wonderful ways to cook duck in this chapter. It's a rich meat that works well in spicier curries. In Indian cuisine, the skin is nearly always removed from duck or any poultry to allow the flavour to penetrate the meat, which makes it lower in fat, too.

As with all poultry, refrigerate it as soon as possible after you have bought it and use it within a day or two of purchase. Duck will keep in the freezer for three months. Thaw in the fridge before cooking.

chicken korma

The sauce in this mild curry is thickened with ground almonds and enriched with coconut milk and cream.

 SERVES 4
READY IN **3½–5½ HOURS ON LOW**

toasted flaked (slivered) almonds	75 g/3 oz/¾ cup
ghee or unsalted (sweet) butter	15 ml/1 tbsp
groundnut (peanut) or sunflower oil	10 ml/2 tsp
onion,	1, chopped
or frozen diced onion	45 ml/3 tbsp
garlic cloves,	2, crushed
or garlic purée (paste)	10 ml/2 tsp
cardamom pods	4
ground cumin	10 ml/2 tsp
ground coriander	5 ml/1 tsp
ground cinnamon	1.5 ml/¼ tsp
ground turmeric	1.5 ml/¼ tsp
salt	2.5 ml/½ tsp
coconut milk	300 ml/½ pint/1¼ cups
chicken fillets	450 g/1 lb, cut into large bite-sized chunks
tomato purée (paste)	5 ml/1 tsp
boiling chicken or vegetable stock	100 ml/3½ fl oz/scant ¾ cup
double (heavy) cream	60 ml/4 tbsp
fresh lime juice	15 ml/1 tbsp
garam masala	5 ml/1 tsp

1 Reserve about a quarter of the almonds for garnishing, then put the rest into a spice grinder or coffee mill and grind until fine.

2 Heat the ghee or butter and the oil in a large frying pan. Fry the onion for 5 minutes until beginning to soften. Add the garlic, cardamom pods, cumin, ground coriander, cinnamon and turmeric and cook for a further minute, stirring. Turn off the heat and stir in the salt and coconut milk.

3 Put the chicken in the ceramic cooking pot and pour over the spice and coconut mixture. Stir the tomato purée into the stock and add that as well. Mix together, cover with the lid and switch the slow cooker on to Low. Cook for 3–5 hours or until the chicken is tender.

4 Stir the cream, lime or lemon juice and garam masala into the curry and cook for a further 30 minutes. Taste and adjust the seasoning if necessary.

5 Serve with Saffron or Turmeric Rice (page 143) and popadoms.

tips

- If you can't find ready-toasted flaked almonds, dry-fry flaked almonds in a non-stick frying pan over a medium heat for 2–3 minutes until just beginning to colour – take care, and keep watch, as they burn easily.

- To contrast the sweetness of the coconut milk, a dash of lemon or lime juice is added in this recipe, but you can leave this out if you prefer.

- For a hotter version, you can add a pinch of dried chilli flakes with the spices.

tandoori chicken

Traditionally cooked in a hot clay oven, a slow cooker won't produce the blackened effect usually associated with this dish.

SERVES 4
READY IN **3–4 HOURS ON LOW**

large chicken portions	4, skinned
garlic cloves,	2, crushed
or garlic purée (paste)	10 ml/2 tsp
ground coriander	10 ml/2 tsp
ground ginger	2.5 ml/½ tsp
ground paprika	30 ml/2 tbsp
garam masala	15 ml/1 tbsp
ground turmeric	2.5 ml/½ tsp
cornflour (cornstarch)	2.5 ml/½ tsp
salt	2.5 ml/½ tsp
lime juice,	45 ml/3 tbsp
or bottled lemon juice	15 ml/1 tbsp
water	30 ml/2 tbsp
thick plain yoghurt	200 ml/7 fl oz/scant 1 cup

1 Make several deep slashes in the chicken to allow the flavours to penetrate. Place in the ceramic cooking pot.

2 Blend together the garlic, ground coriander, ginger, paprika, garam masala, turmeric, cornflour, salt and lime or lemon juice and water to make a smooth paste. Stir in the yoghurt.

3 Spoon and spread the spice mixture all over the chicken, then cover the slow cooker with the lid and switch on to Low.

4 Cook for 3–4 hours or until the chicken is cooked and very tender. Lift out of the juices with a draining spoon.

5 Serve with a finely shredded lettuce, cucumber and onion salad or plain rice and chutney.

tip

● Use the tandoori mix with other meats or fish. This tasty chicken curry is really low in fat, yet full of flavour and you can use your favourite curry powder or paste.

chicken with spinach & lentils

This tasty chicken curry is really low in fat, yet full of flavour. Lentils are used to thicken the rich-tasting sauce.

SERVES 4
READY IN **5½ HOURS ON LOW** ①

curry powder or paste	30 ml/2 tbsp
hot (not boiling) chicken or vegetable stock	375 ml/13 fl oz/1½ cups
bay leaf	1
red lentils	75 g/3 oz/scant ½ cup
chicken thighs	8, skinned
salt and freshly ground black pepper	
fresh spinach leaves	200 g/7 oz
chopped fresh or thawed frozen coriander (cilantro)	30 ml/2 tbsp

1 Put the curry powder or paste into the ceramic cooking pot. Add a little of the stock and stir until blended, then stir in the remaining stock. Add the bay leaf.

2 Put the lentils in a sieve (strainer) and rinse under cold running water. Drain, then tip into the cooking pot. Cover with the lid and cook on Low for 3 hours.

3 Season the chicken thighs with salt and pepper and place in a single layer on top of the lentils. Replace the lid and cook for a further 2 hours or until the chicken is just tender.

4 Meanwhile, finely shred the spinach. Add to the ceramic pot, gently pressing it down into the hot stock. Cover and cook for a further 30–45 minutes or until the spinach has wilted and is tender. Taste and adjust the seasoning if necessary.

5 Serve sprinkled with chopped coriander on a bed of white or brown basmati rice.

tip

- Shredded fresh spinach enhances the dish, but you will need a large slow cooker for this. If yours has a capacity less than 3.5 litres/6 pints/15 cups, make this with thawed and drained frozen spinach.

saffron-scented chicken

Saffron is known as the 'royal spice' in India and is used on special occasions. Although expensive, a little goes a long way.

SERVES 4
READY IN **3–4 HOURS ON LOW**   ①

4 skinless chicken breasts	
groundnut (peanut) or sunflower oil	15ml/1 tbsp
fennel seeds	5 ml/1 tsp
onion,	1, chopped
or frozen diced onion	45 ml/3 tbsp
garlic cloves,	2, crushed
or garlic purée (paste)	10 ml/2 tsp
korma curry paste	60 ml/4 tbsp
saffron strands	a pinch
honey	5 ml/1 tsp
very hot (not boiling) chicken or vegetable stock	250 ml/8 fl oz/1 cup
cornflour (cornstarch)	2.5 ml/½ tsp
double (heavy) cream	30 ml/2 tbsp
thick plain yoghurt	150 ml/¼ pint/⅔ cup
salt	to taste
toasted flaked (slivered) almonds	50 g/2 oz/½ cup

1 Cut each chicken breast into three chunks and place in the ceramic cooking pot. Heat the oil in a frying pan, add the fennel seeds and cook for a few seconds, until they begin to sizzle.

2 Add the onion to the pan and cook for 6–7 minutes until almost soft. Stir in the garlic and korma paste and cook for 1 more minute, stirring. Turn off the heat.

3 Stir in the saffron, honey and stock, then tip the mixture over the chicken. Blend the cornflour with the cream, then stir in the yoghurt. Add to the cooking pot and mix well. Add salt to taste.

4 Cover with the lid and cook on Low for 3–4 hours or until the chicken is cooked and tender. Sprinkle with toasted almonds.

5 Serve with rice or naan bread, Sweet Mango Chutney (page 156) and a green vegetable.

tip

- You can use turmeric if you don't have saffron, but it is not an exact equivalent.

chicken with cashew sauce

Making a curry with a nut paste is a classic style of cooking that came from the Moghuls, centuries ago.

SERVES 4

READY IN **4–5 HOURS ON LOW** ①

unsalted cashew nuts	50 g/2 oz/½ cup
large onion,	1, chopped
or frozen diced onion	60 ml/4 tbsp
garlic clove,	1, crushed
or garlic purée (paste)	5 ml/1 tsp
tomato purée (paste)	15 ml/1 tbsp
lemon juice	15 ml/1 tbsp
cold water	15 ml/1 tbsp
garam masala	5 ml/1 tsp
chilli powder	5 ml/1 tsp
ground turmeric	2.5 ml/½ tsp
salt	2.5 ml/½ tsp
chicken breast fillets	400 g/14 oz, cut into bite-sized chunks
groundnut (peanut) or sunflower oil	30 ml/2 tbsp
baby button mushrooms	225 g/8 oz
very hot (not boiling) chicken stock	300 ml/½ pint/1¼ cups
chopped fresh or thawed frozen coriander (cilantro)	45 ml/3 tbsp

1 Put the cashew nuts, onion, garlic, tomato purée, lemon juice, water, garam masala, chilli, turmeric and salt into a food processor and blend to a fairly smooth paste, adding a little more water if necessary.

2 Place the chicken in the ceramic pot. Heat 15 ml/1 tbsp of the oil in a large frying pan, add the mushrooms and fry for 2–3 minutes or until lightly browned. Lift out of the pan with a slotted spoon, leaving any juices behind.

3 Add the remaining 15 ml/1 tbsp of oil to the frying pan. Spoon in the nut paste, turn down the heat and gently fry for 3–4 minutes. Turn off the heat, then stir in the stock. Tip into the ceramic pot, then gently stir to mix everything together.

4 Cover with the lid and switch the slow cooker on to Low. Cook for 4–5 hours, stirring halfway through cooking time, if possible, until the chicken is tender and the sauce fairly thick. Stir in the coriander at the end and adjust the seasoning, if needed.

5 Serve with basmati rice and Sweet Mango Chutney (page 156).

tip

● Make sure you use unsalted cashews.

northern chicken curry

Cooking chicken on the bone adds flavour and succulence. Use chicken pieces such as drumsticks or thighs and remove the skins.

SERVES 4
READY IN **4–6 HOURS ON LOW** ②

chicken drumsticks or thighs	8
plain (all-purpose) flour	15 ml/1 tbsp
salt and freshly ground black pepper	
groundnut (peanut) or sunflower oil	45 ml/3 tbsp
whole cloves	4
green cardamom pods	4, split
cinnamon stick	½
large onion,	1, chopped
or frozen diced onion	60 ml/4 tbsp
garlic cloves,	3, crushed
or garlic purée (paste)	15 ml/1 tbsp
grated fresh or bottled ginger	15 ml/1 tbsp
chilli powder	5 ml/1 tsp
ground turmeric	5 ml/1 tsp
ground coriander	15 ml/1 tbsp
can of chopped tomatoes	200 g/7 oz/small
very hot (not boiling) chicken or vegetable stock	450 ml/¾ pint/2 cups
garam masala	5 ml/1 tsp

1 Remove the skin from the chicken pieces, rinse under cold water and pat dry with kitchen paper (paper towels). Season the flour with salt and pepper and use to dust the chicken lightly. Heat 30 ml/2 tbsp of the oil in a large frying pan and fry the chicken until browned on all sides. Lift out of the pan with a slotted spoon, leaving any fat and juices behind and transfer to the ceramic cooking pot.

2 Add the remaining oil to the pan. Fry the cloves, cardamom pods and cinnamon stick for a few seconds until aromatic. Add the onion and fry for 5–6 minutes until beginning to colour, then stir in the garlic, ginger, chilli, turmeric and ground coriander. Cook for a further minute.

3 Turn off the heat, then stir in the tomatoes and stock. Pour over the chicken pieces, cover with the lid and cook on Low for 4–6 hours, or until the chicken is cooked and very tender.

4 Lift the chicken pieces on to serving plates. Stir the garam masala into the sauce, then taste and adjust the seasoning, if necessary. Spoon the sauce over the chicken.

5 Serve with Mushroom Pilau (page 144) or Lemon-scented Rice (page 143).

tip

- Meaning 'warming spice mix', garam masala can be added at the start of cooking, but is more usually stirred in at the end. It contains a mixture of cassia leaf, black pepper, coriander, cumin, chilli, cardamom, cloves, fennel, mace and nutmeg.

chicken mangalore

Although food from Southern India is often hot and fiery, this is a medium curry. Lemon-scented Rice is a great accompaniment.

 SERVES 4
READY IN **4–6 HOURS ON LOW** ②

chicken drumsticks or thighs	8
desiccated coconut	75 ml/5 tbsp
groundnut (peanut) or sunflower oil	30 ml/2 tbsp
onion,	1, chopped
or frozen diced onion	60 ml/4 tbsp
garlic cloves,	3, crushed
or garlic purée (paste)	15 ml/1 tbsp
grated fresh or bottled ginger	15 ml/1 tbsp
coriander seeds	15 ml/1 tbsp
whole cloves	4
ground cinnamon	1.5 ml/¼ tsp
red chillies,	1–2, seeded and finely chopped
or red chilli purée (paste)	5–10 ml/1–2 tsp
Tomatoes	4, roughly chopped
very hot (not boiling) chicken or vegetable stock	400 ml/14 fl oz/1¾ cups
salt and freshly ground black pepper	

1 Remove the skins from the chicken pieces, rinse under cold water and pat dry. Place in a single layer in the ceramic cooking pot.

2 Put the coconut in a dry non-stick frying pan and gently toast over a medium heat for a few minutes until golden, stirring all the time. Tip on to a plate.

3 Add the oil to the pan and fry the onion for 6–7 minutes, until beginning to soften. Add the garlic, ginger, coriander seeds, cloves, cinnamon and chillies and cook for 2 minutes, stirring frequently.

4 Turn off the heat and stir in about half of the toasted coconut along with all of the tomatoes and stock. Pour over the chicken. Season with salt and pepper.

5 Cover with the lid and cook on High for 2–3 hours or on Low for 4–6 hours or until the chicken is thoroughly cooked and tender. Check the seasoning again. Sprinkle with the rest of the coconut.

6 Serve with Lemon-scented Rice (page 143).

tip

- As an alternative, you could serve this with naan bread and steamed spinach.

chicken with red lentils

This is a simplified version of 'Dhanzak', popular among the Parsi community where it is often made on Sundays.

SERVES 4
READY IN **4–6 HOURS ON LOW**

groundnut (peanut) or sunflower oil	15ml/1 tbsp
large onion,	1, chopped
or frozen diced onion	60 ml/4 tbsp
garlic clove,	1, crushed
or garlic purée (paste)	5 ml/1 tsp
green chilli,	1, seeded and finely chopped
or green chilli purée (paste)	5 ml/1 tsp
chilli powder	2.5 ml/½ tsp
ground turmeric	5 ml/1 tsp
ground coriander	5 ml/1 tsp
ground cumin	5 ml/1 tsp
soft brown sugar	5 ml/1 tsp
wine vinegar	15 ml/1 tbsp
can of chopped tomatoes	200 g/7 oz/small
skinless chicken breasts	4, each cut into 3 large pieces
red lentils	175 g/6 oz/1 cup
large potatoes	2, peeled and cut into 4 cm/1½ in chunks
very hot (not boiling) chicken or vegetable stock	750 ml/1¼ pints/3 cups
salt and freshly ground black pepper	
garam masala	10 ml/2 tsp
chopped fresh or frozen coriander (cilantro)	30 ml/2 tbsp

1 Heat the oil in a large frying pan and gently cook the onion for 7–8 minutes until almost soft. Stir in the garlic, green chilli and chilli powder, turmeric, ground coriander and cumin. Cook for a further minute, stirring all the time.

2 Add the sugar, vinegar and tomatoes to the pan and gently heat for a few minutes. Tip the mixture into the ceramic cooking pot.

3 Add the chicken, lentils and potatoes to the pot and stir. Pour in the stock and season with a little salt and pepper. Mix everything together, then cover with the lid and switch on the slow cooker.

4 Cook on High for 2–3 hours or Low for 4–6 hours or until everything is tender and the lentils have soaked up most of the stock to make a thick sauce.

5 Stir in the garam masala and chopped coriander, then check the seasoning again.

6 Serve with brown rice and sweet Indian pickles.

variation

● For a prawn (shrimp) dhanzak, leave out the chicken and substitute 400 g/14 oz large raw prawns, thawed if frozen and drained in a sieve (strainer), for just the last 45 minutes of cooking time.

chicken biryani

This dish has minimal preparation as it uses canned caramelised onions, curry paste and ready-toasted cashew nuts.

SERVES 4

READY IN **1–1¼ HOURS ON HIGH**   ②

can of fried onions in olive oil	400 g/14 oz/large
garlic cloves,	2, crushed
or garlic purée (paste)	10 ml/2 tsp
biryani curry paste	30 ml/2 tbsp
very hot (not boiling) chicken stock	1 litre/1¾ pints/4¼ cups
chicken breast	700 g/1½ lb, diced or cut into thin strips
small florets of fresh or frozen cauliflower	300 g/11 oz, thawed
frozen peas	200 g/7 oz/8 tbsp, thawed
easy-cook (converted) rice	300 g/11 oz/1½ cups
salt and freshly ground black pepper	
unsalted toasted cashew nuts	150 g/5 oz/1½ cups
chopped fresh or thawed frozen coriander (cilantro)	60 ml/4 tbsp

1 Put the onions, garlic and curry paste in the ceramic cooking pot. Pour in a small amount of the stock and stir until the curry paste is blended, then stir in the rest of the stock.

2 Add the chicken, cauliflower, peas and rice and season to taste with salt and pepper. Stir, then cover with the lid and switch on the slow cooker to High.

3 Cook for 1–1¼ hours or until the chicken is cooked through and the rice is tender and has absorbed most of the stock.

4 Stir the nuts and fresh coriander into the rice.

5 Spoon on to warmed plates and serve straight away while hot, topped with a spoonful of thick plain yoghurt along with a large pile of popadoms.

tips

- If you prefer, less expensive unsalted roasted peanuts may be used instead of the cashews.

- If you can't find canned fried onions, prepare your own by frying 2 finely sliced onions in 30 ml/2 tbsp light olive oil over a low heat for 12–15 minutes, stirring frequently until lightly browned.

chicken jalfrezi

This fairly hot curry is cooked for a relatively short time in the slow cooker, to retain the freshness of the tomatoes and pepper.

SERVES 4
READY IN **4 HOURS ON LOW**

groundnut (peanut) or sunflower oil	45 ml/3 tbsp
skinned boneless chicken thighs	8, halved
large onion,	1, chopped
or frozen diced onion	60 ml/2 tbsp
garlic cloves,	2, crushed
or garlic purée (paste)	10 ml/2 tsp
grated fresh or bottled ginger	15 ml/1 tbsp
ground coriander	5 ml/1 tsp
ground cumin	5 ml/1 tsp
ground turmeric	5 ml/1 tsp
ground cinnamon	1.5 ml/¼ tsp
ground cloves	1.5 ml/¼ tsp
very hot (not boiling) chicken or vegetable stock	150 ml/¼ pint/⅔ cup
green (bell) pepper	1, halved, seeded and sliced
tomatoes	6, roughly chopped
salt	to taste
chopped fresh or thawed frozen coriander (cilantro)	45 ml/3 tbsp
thick plain or Greek-style yoghurt (optional)	75 ml/5 tbsp

1 Heat 15 ml/1 tbsp of the oil in a pan and fry the chicken for 2–3 minutes, turning until beginning to brown in places. Transfer to the ceramic cooking pot.

2 Add the remaining oil to the pan and fry the onion for 7–8 minutes, until almost soft. Add the garlic, ginger, ground coriander, cumin, turmeric, cinnamon and cloves. Cook, stirring, for 1 minute.

3 Turn off the heat and stir in the stock. Tip the mixture over the chicken, then add the green pepper and tomatoes and season with a little salt. Stir well.

4 Cover with the lid and cook on High for 2 hours or on Low for 4 hours. Stir in the chopped coriander, then taste and adjust the seasoning, if necessary. For a creamy sauce, stir in the yoghurt.

5 Serve with basmati rice.

tip

- Chicken thighs are less expensive than breast and are excellent in curries.

- For a creamy finish, stir in yoghurt at the end of cooking.

butter chicken

Known as Murgh Makhani, this has a buttery smooth sauce thickened with ground cashews and cream.

SERVES 4
READY IN **4–6 HOURS ON LOW**

unsalted cashew nuts	100 g/4 oz/1 cup
medium curry powder	30 ml/2 tbsp
garlic cloves,	3, peeled
or garlic purée (paste)	15 ml/1 tbsp
grated fresh or bottled ginger	10 ml/2 tsp
tomato purée (paste)	15 ml/1 tbsp
chilli powder	5 ml/1 tsp
ground cinnamon	1.5 ml/¼ tsp
thick plain yoghurt	150 ml/¼ pint/⅔ cup
ghee or unsalted (sweet) butter	45 ml/3 tbsp
boneless skinless chicken thighs	8
onion,	1, chopped
or frozen diced onion	60 ml/4 tbsp
green cardamom pods	4, split
red or white wine vinegar	15 ml/1 tbsp
can of chopped tomatoes	400 g/14 oz/large
boiling chicken stock	150 ml/¼ pint/⅔ cup
salt and freshly ground black pepper	
double (heavy) cream	60 ml/4 tbsp

1 In a non-stick frying pan, dry-roast the cashews over a low heat for 2 minutes. Sprinkle over the curry powder and cook for a further 1–2 minutes, stirring all the time until the cashews are just beginning to turn golden.

2 Tip into a spice or coffee mill and grind to a powder. In a blender, process the ground cashew nuts, garlic, ginger, tomato purée, chilli powder, cinnamon and half the yoghurt to a smooth paste. Add the rest of the yoghurt and briefly blend again.

3 Melt half the ghee or butter in a large saucepan and fry the chicken thighs for a minute or two on each side until golden. Transfer to the ceramic cooking pot.

4 Put the rest of the ghee or butter, the onions and cardamoms into the pan and fry for 7–8 minutes until the onions begin to soften. Stir in the vinegar. Tip the mixture over the chicken thighs in the cooking pot.

5 Mix the tomatoes, stock and a little salt and pepper together, then pour into the cooking pot. Cover with the lid and cook on High for 2–3 hours or Low for 4–6 hours, until the chicken is tender.

6 Lift the chicken on to warmed serving plates. Stir the cream into the sauce, then taste and add more seasoning if necessary.

7 Serve with plain boiled basmati rice and a side salad or green vegetable.

tip

- If you have a can of whole tomatoes, simply remove the top and chop roughly in the can.

spiced duck

Long, gentle simmering in the slow cooker makes duck portions so tender and succulent that the meat falls off the bone.

SERVES 4

READY IN 6 HOURS ON LOW   ①

whole coriander seeds	30 ml/2 tbsp
cumin seeds	10 ml/2 tsp
duck portions	4, skinned
groundnut (peanut) or sunflower oil	30 ml/2 tbsp
onions,	2, chopped
or frozen diced onion	90 ml/6 tbsp
grated fresh or bottled ginger	15 ml/1 tbsp
garlic cloves,	2, crushed
or garlic purée (paste)	10 ml/2 tsp
whole cloves	6
ground cinnamon	2.5 ml/½ tsp
hot chilli powder	5 ml/1 tsp
jaggery or muscovado sugar	10 ml/2 tsp
red wine vinegar	15 ml/1 tbsp
very hot (not boiling) chicken or vegetable stock	250 ml/8 fl oz/1 cup
salt	to taste
thick plain or Greek yoghurt	60 ml/4 tbsp
chopped fresh or frozen coriander (cilantro)	60 ml/4 tbsp

1 Process the coriander seeds and cumin seeds in a spice or coffee grinder until finely ground. Alternatively, crush them with a pestle and mortar or in a bowl, using the end of a wooden rolling pin.

2 Pack the duck into the slow cooker in a single layer, as snugly as possible. Heat the oil in a pan and fry the onions for 7–8 minutes, until almost soft. Stir in the ginger, garlic, cloves, cinnamon, chilli and jaggery or sugar and cook for a further minute, stirring.

3 Turn off the heat, then stir in vinegar, followed by the stock. Season with a little salt and pour over the duck.

4 Cover with the lid and cook on High for 3 hours or on Low for 6 hours or until the duck is very tender.

5 Lift the duck on to warmed serving plates. Stir a little of the hot sauce into the yoghurt, then stir this mixture into the sauce with the chopped coriander. Taste and adjust the seasoning, if necessary.

6 Spoon the sauce over the duck and serve with Lemon-scented (page 143) or plain basmati rice.

coconut duck curry

As duck is quite a fatty meat, it's important to remove the skin and fat before you cook it in order to get the best results.

SERVES 4
READY IN **6 HOURS ON LOW** ①

duck portions, skinned	4
curry leaves	6
fresh coconut	150 g/5 oz, grated
groundnut (peanut) or sunflower oil	15 ml/1 tbsp
onion,	1, sliced
or frozen diced onion	45 ml/3 tbsp
grated fresh or bottled ginger	15 ml/1 tbsp
garlic cloves,	2, crushed
or garlic purée (paste)	10 ml/2 tsp
mild curry powder	30 ml/2 tbsp
ground coriander	10 ml/2 tsp
ground turmeric	5 ml/1 tsp
mild chilli powder	5 ml/1 tsp
ground cinnamon	5 ml/1 tsp
coconut milk	400 ml/14 oz/large can
boiling vegetable or chicken stock	175 ml/6 fl oz/¾ cup
salt and freshly ground black pepper	
chopped fresh or frozen coriander (cilantro)	60 ml/4 tbsp

1 Pack the duck into the slow cooker in a single layer, as snugly as possible. Tuck the curry leaves in between the portions and sprinkle over about half of the grated coconut.

2 Heat the oil in a pan and fry the onion for 6–7 minutes until almost soft. Mix in the ginger, garlic, curry powder, ground coriander, turmeric, chilli and cinnamon and cook for a further minute, stirring. Turn off the heat, then stir in the coconut milk and stock. Season with a little salt and pour the mixture over the duck portions.

3 Cover with the lid and cook on High for 3 hours or on Low for 6 hours or until the duck is very tender.

4 Lift the duck portions on to warmed plates. Stir the chopped coriander into the sauce, taste and adjust the seasoning if necessary.

5 Garnish with the remaining grated coconut and serve with basmati or Saffron Rice (page 143).

tip

- Curry leaves are often used in southern Indian cooking and are picked from the curry tree. They have a distinct flavour and aroma and can be bought fresh or dried; the fresh ones can be frozen.

royal duck biryani

Biryanis are traditionally served topped with golden fried onions. These are cooked early in this recipe, but can be quickly reheated.

SERVES 4
READY IN **6 HOURS ON LOW**

duck breasts, skinned	4
garlic cloves, or garlic purée (paste)	3, crushed 15 ml/1 tbsp
grated fresh or bottled ginger	10 ml/2 tsp
thick plain or Greek-style yoghurt	150 ml/¼ pint/⅔ cup
groundnut (peanut) or sunflower oil	30 ml/2 tbsp
ghee or unsalted (sweet) butter	15 ml/1 tbsp
onions	2, thinly sliced
medium curry powder	30 ml/2 tbsp
cumin seeds	10 ml/2 tsp
whole cloves	6
black peppercorns	6
green cardamom pods	6, split
can of chopped tomatoes	200 g/7 oz/small
very hot (not boiling) chicken or vegetable stock	200 ml/7 fl oz/scant 1 cup
basmati rice	350 g/12 oz/1½ cups
saffron threads	5 ml/1 tsp
hot milk	45 ml/3 tbsp
salt and freshly ground black pepper	

1 Cut the duck into large chunks. Mix the garlic, ginger and yoghurt in a large bowl, add the duck and stir well. Cover and leave for 30 minutes at room temperature or in the fridge for up to 6 hours, if preferred.

2 Heat 15 ml/1 tbsp of the oil with the ghee or butter in a frying pan and gently cook the onions for 10 minutes, until soft and beginning to turn golden. Transfer half of the onions to the ceramic cooking pot. Cook the rest of the onions for a further 4–5 minutes, stirring frequently until a rich golden brown colour. Transfer to another bowl and set aside.

3 Remove the duck from the marinade. Heat the rest of the oil in the frying pan and brown the duck on all sides. Lift out of the pan with a draining spoon, leaving the juices behind, and add to the pot.

4 Fry the curry powder, cumin seeds, cloves, peppercorns and cardamom pods in the pan juices for 30 seconds, stirring. Turn off the heat and stir in the tomatoes and stock. Pour over the duck.

5 Cover and cook on High for 3 hours or Low for 6 hours. Towards the end of cooking, cook the rice according to the packet instructions. Drain well. While the rice is cooking, infuse the saffron in the hot milk for 10 minutes.

6 Lift the duck portions on to a warmed plate. Gently stir the rice into the sauce. Taste and adjust the seasoning if necessary. Spoon on to plates, then place a portion of duck on top of each. Drizzle with the saffron milk, then spoon over the reserved fried onion.

7 Serve with a green salad and Sweet Mango Chutney (page 156).

lamb

Along with chicken, lamb is a very popular meat in India and this is reflected by a huge number of flavoursome lamb dishes, all of which convert very well to the slow cooker.

Some of the most popular lamb curries include lamb madras, rogan josh and dopiaza to name but a few. Generally, the best cuts of lamb for slow cooker curries are shoulder and neck, as they are wonderfully tender after long slow cooking, but you can use leg of lamb if you prefer. In India the bones are often left in the meat as they add to the flavour of the sauce; if you do this you will need almost double the amount of meat given in the recipe.

Goat is also widely eaten throughout India; I haven't featured any recipes for this, but it can be used instead of lamb in any of these dishes.

lamb korma

Korma is one of the mildest curries and therefore ideal for those who don't like their food too spicy.

SERVES 4

READY IN **6 HOURS ON LOW** ①

groundnut (peanut) or sunflower oil	30 ml/2 tbsp
lean lamb	700 g/1½ lb, trimmed and cut into cubes
large onion,	1, finely chopped
or frozen diced onion	60 ml/4 tbsp
garlic cloves,	2, crushed
or garlic purée (paste)	10 ml/2 tsp
grated fresh or bottled ginger	10 ml/2 tsp
ground almonds	50 g/2 oz/½ cup
very hot (not boiling) lamb or vegetable stock	250 ml/8 fl oz/1 cup
green cardamom pods	3, split
ground cumin	5 ml/1 tsp
ground coriander	5 ml/1 tsp
mild chilli powder	2.5 ml/½ tsp
ground cinnamon	2.5 ml/½ tsp
caster (superfine) sugar	2.5 ml/½ tsp
salt and freshly ground black pepper	
garam masala	2.5 ml/½ tsp
thick plain yoghurt or single (light) cream	60 ml/4 tbsp

1 Heat 20 ml/4 tsp of the oil in a large frying pan, add the meat and fry until browned all over. Transfer to the ceramic cooking pot with a slotted spoon, leaving most of the oil and juices behind. Add the remaining oil to the pan and cook the onion for 4–5 minutes, stirring until it begins to colour.

2 In a bowl, blend the garlic, ginger and ground almonds with 75 ml/5 tbsp of the stock. Add the cardamom, cumin, ground coriander, chilli powder, cinnamon and sugar to the pan and stir for a minute, then stir in the almond mixture and cook for a further minute. Turn off the heat and stir in the rest of the stock, then tip the mixture over the lamb in the ceramic cooking pot.

3 Season to taste with salt and pepper. Cover and cook on High for 3 hours or on Low for 6 hours until the lamb is very tender.

4 Stir in the garam masala and yoghurt or cream, taste and adjust the seasoning if necessary.

5 Serve with Tarka Dhal (page 152) or Lemon-scented Rice (page 143).

tip

- Bags of frozen diced onion are a great freezer standby as you can simply tip out what you need and return the rest to the freezer.

indian lamb with spiced lentils

Although it is a little time-consuming, grinding your own spices adds a unique flavour to this delicious curry.

SERVES 4
READY IN **6–7 HOURS ON LOW**   ②

green lentils	225 g/8 oz/1¼ cups
green cardamom pods	8, seeds reserved and pods discarded
cumin seeds	15 ml/1 tbsp
black peppercorns	4
groundnut (peanut) or sunflower oil	30 ml/2 tbsp
large onion,	1, sliced
or frozen diced onion	60 ml/2 tbsp
garlic cloves,	2, crushed
or garlic purée (paste)	10 ml/2 tsp
grated fresh or bottled ginger	30 ml/2 tbsp
ground turmeric	5 ml/1 tsp
ground cinnamon	2.5 ml/½ tsp
dried red chilli,	a pinch
or red chilli purée (paste)	5 ml/1 tsp
lean boneless leg of lamb	450 g/1lb, trimmed and cut into cubes
very hot (not boiling) lamb stock	600 ml/1 pint/2½ cups
plum tomatoes	6, roughly chopped
fresh or bottled lemon juice	15 ml/1 tbsp
chopped fresh or frozen coriander (cilantro)	45 ml/3 tbsp

1 Rinse the lentils in a sieve (strainer) under cold running water, then tip them into a bowl. Cover with cold water and leave to soak for several minutes while preparing the rest of the ingredients.

2 Crush the cardamom seeds and cumin seeds and peppercorns in a pestle and mortar or grind them in a spice or coffee grinder. Heat the oil in a large frying pan and fry the onion for 7–8 minutes or until almost soft. Add the garlic, ginger, turmeric, cinnamon, chilli and crushed spices and cook for a further minute or two, stirring all the time. Scrape the mixture into the ceramic cooking pot.

3 Add the lamb, stock, tomatoes and lemon juice to the cooking pot. Drain the lentils and add them as well. Stir everything together. Cover with the lid and cook on High for 3–3½ hours or Low for 6–7 hours until very tender.

4 Stir in the chopped coriander and serve with Saffron Rice (page 143) and Sweet Mango Chutney (page 156).

variation

● This curry is equally good made with beef, but it would need a slightly longer cooking time.

aromatic lamb

Known as kashmiri tamatari ghosht, this is a mild dish with fragrant spices that don't dominate the flavour of the lamb.

SERVES 4
READY IN **6-8 HOURS ON LOW**   ①

sunflower oil	15 ml/1 tbsp
cumin seeds	5 ml/1 tsp
onion,	1, thinly sliced
or frozen diced onion	45 ml/ 3 tbsp
ground turmeric	5 ml/1 tsp
whole cloves	3
ground cinnamon	5 ml/1 tsp
bay leaf	1
lean boneless lamb	700 g/1½ lb, cut into chunks
garlic clove,	1, crushed
or garlic purée (paste)	5 ml/1 tsp
grated fresh or bottled ginger	10 ml/2 tsp
large potatoes	2, about 450 g/1 lb, peeled and cut into chunks
can of chopped tomatoes	400 g/14 oz/large
hot (not boiling) lamb or vegetable stock	300 ml/½ pint/1¼ cups
salt and freshly ground black pepper	

1 Heat the oil in a heavy-based frying pan and sprinkle in the cumin seeds. When they start to pop, add the onion, turmeric, cloves, cinnamon and bay leaf and cook gently for 1–2 minutes, stirring.

2 Add the lamb and fry for about 5 minutes until the meat is lightly browned on all sides. Add the garlic and ginger and cook for 1 minute, stirring continuously.

3 Transfer the lamb mixture to the ceramic cooking pot and switch the slow cooker to Low. Stir in the potatoes, tomatoes and stock, then season with salt and pepper.

4 Cover with the lid and cook for 6–8 hours or until the lamb and vegetables are very tender.

5 Serve the lamb drizzled with yoghurt and scattered with chopped coriander.

tip

- As the lamb is cooked slowly, you can use any cut, so there is no need to buy an expensive one.

lamb dopiaza

Dopiaza broadly translates as 'two onions' or 'double onions' and here they are used both as the base and as a finishing garnish.

SERVES 4
READY IN **6 HOURS ON LOW**   ②

large onions	3
garlic cloves,	2, crushed
or garlic purée (paste)	10 ml/2 tsp
grated fresh or bottled ginger	30 ml/2 tbsp
cumin seeds	5 ml/1 tsp
coriander seeds	5 ml/1 tsp
black mustard seeds	5 ml/1 tsp
crushed dried chillies	1.5–2.5 ml/¼–½ tsp
lamb or vegetable stock or water	200 ml/7 fl oz/scant 1 cup
ghee or unsalted (sweet) butter	30 ml/2 tbsp
groundnut (peanut) or sunflower oil	30 ml/2 tbsp
lean diced lamb	700 g/1½ lb
cornflour (cornstarch)	2.5 ml/½ tsp
thick plain yoghurt	120 ml/4 fl oz/½ cup
whole cloves	4
green cardamom pods	4, split
salt and freshly ground black pepper	
garam masala	5 ml/1 tsp

1 Roughly chop one of the onions and put in a food processor with the garlic, ginger, cumin, coriander and mustard seeds and chillies. Add 30 ml/2 tbsp of the stock or water and process until finely chopped. Blend in a further 60 ml/4 tbsp of the stock or water.

2 Heat 15 ml/1 tbsp of the ghee or butter and 15 ml/1 tbsp of the oil in a large frying pan. Fry the lamb in batches until browned all over. Transfer to the ceramic cooking pot using a slotted spoon, leaving the fat and juices behind.

3 Add the spice paste to the frying pan and fry, stirring for 1 minute. Stir in the remaining stock or water. In a separate bowl, blend the cornflour with a little of the yoghurt, then stir in the rest of the yoghurt. Stir into the spice mixture in the frying pan.

4 Pour the contents of the pan over the lamb, add the cloves and cardamom pods and season with salt and pepper. Stir, then cover with the lid. Cook on High for 3 hours or Low for 6.

5 Towards the end of cooking time, finely slice the remaining onions. Heat the rest of the ghee or butter and oil in a frying pan and cook the onions for about 10 minutes, stirring frequently until golden and soft.

6 When the curry has cooked, stir in the garam masala, then taste and adjust the seasoning if necessary.

7 Serve scattered with the fried onions along with basmati rice and Indian chutney.

tip

- The whole spices are always left in the curry, to be removed by the diners.

rogan josh

There are many different versions of this dish; this one is very simple and uses ready-made curry paste.

SERVES 4
READY IN **6 HOURS ON LOW** ③

groundnut (peanut) or sunflower oil	30 ml/2 tbsp
lean diced lamb	700 g/1½ lb
onions,	2, chopped
or frozen diced onions	90 ml/6 tbsp
garlic cloves,	2, crushed
or garlic purée (paste)	10 ml/2 tsp
grated fresh or bottled ginger	15 ml/1 tbsp
Madras curry paste	45 ml/3 tbsp
paprika	10 ml/2 tsp
green cardamom pods	6, split
whole cloves	4
bay leaves	2
tomato purée (paste)	30 ml/2 tbsp
very hot (not boiling) lamb or vegetable stock	250 ml/8 fl oz/1 cup
salt and freshly ground black pepper	
cornflour (cornstarch)	2.5 ml/½ tsp
thick plain yoghurt	175 ml/6 fl oz/¾ cup

1 Heat 15 ml/1 tbsp of the oil in a large non-stick frying pan. Add the lamb and fry over a high heat for 3–4 minutes, until browned all over. Lift out with a slotted spoon, leaving the juices behind, and transfer to the ceramic cooking pot.

2 Add the remaining 15 ml/1 tbsp oil to the pan, then gently cook the onions for 6–7 minutes until beginning to soften. Stir in the garlic, ginger, curry paste, paprika, cardamom and cloves. Cook for a further minute, stirring all the time.

3 Add the bay leaves and tomato purée, then slowly stir in the stock. Season with salt and pepper. Heat until steaming hot, but not boiling, then pour over the lamb in the pot.

4 In a separate bowl, blend the cornflour with a little of the yoghurt, then stir in the rest of the yoghurt. Gradually stir into the lamb mixture. Cover with the lid and cook on High for 3 hours or Low for 6 hours until really tender.

5 Taste and adjust seasoning if necessary, before serving with plain basmati rice or Mushroom Pilau (page 144).

tip

- Keep curry paste in the fridge once opened and use before the use-by date for the best flavour.

lamb parsi

A similar dish to biryani, here the lamb is marinated in yoghurt, a traditional technique in parsi cuisine.

SERVES 4
READY IN **6 HOURS ON LOW**   ②

cornflour (cornstarch)	2.5 ml/½ tsp
garlic cloves,	2, crushed
or garlic purée (paste)	10 ml/2 tsp
ground cumin	10 ml/2 tsp
ground coriander	5 ml/1 tsp
cayenne pepper	5 ml/1 tsp
garam masala	10 ml/2 tsp
Greek-style yoghurt	300 ml/½ pint/1¼ cups
lean lamb	700 g/1½ lb, trimmed and diced
ghee or unsalted (sweet) butter	30 ml/2 tbsp
groundnut (peanut) or sunflower oil	15ml/1 tbsp
large onion,	1, sliced
or frozen diced onion	60 ml/2 tbsp
potatoes	350 g/12 oz, peeled and cut into large chunks
salt and freshly ground black pepper	
hot (not boiling) lamb or vegetable stock	400 ml/14 fl oz/1¾ cups
basmati rice	350 g/12 oz/1½ cups

1 Make the marinade in a large bowl by mixing the cornflour, garlic, cumin, ground coriander, cayenne pepper, garam masala and about 30 ml/2 tbsp of the yoghurt together. Stir in the rest of the yoghurt. Add the lamb, stir to coat, then cover and leave to marinate in the fridge for 2–3 hours or overnight if you prefer.

2 Heat half the ghee or butter and 5 ml/1 tsp of the oil in a large frying pan. Add the onion and fry for 7–8 minutes or until almost soft. Transfer to the ceramic cooking pot with a slotted spoon.

3 Remove the lamb from the marinade. Add the rest of the ghee and oil to the pan, then fry the lamb in batches until evenly browned, transferring each batch to the ceramic cooking pot. Tip the potatoes in on top of the lamb, season with a little salt and pepper and stir everything together.

4 Add a little of the stock to the frying pan and swirl to dissolve any sediment. Tip into the ceramic pot. Blend the remaining marinade with the rest of the stock and add to the pot as well. Stir again.

5 Cover with the lid and cook on High for 3 hours or on Low for 6 hours. Towards the end of cooking time, cook the rice according to the packet directions. Drain well and fork through the cooked meat and sauce.

6 Serve with popadoms, salad and Cucumber and Coriander Raita (page 158).

tip

- With this type of dish, cooking the rice separately, then stirring it into the finished dish, ensures that the grains stay fluffy.

spicy lamb with sweet potatoes

Sweet potatoes are grown in many parts of India and their flavour goes beautifully with lamb. Here they help to thicken the sauce.

SERVES 4
READY IN **6 HOURS ON LOW**   ②

groundnut (peanut) or sunflower oil	30 ml/2 tbsp
onions,	2, sliced
or frozen diced onion	90 ml/6 tbsp
lean boneless lamb	700 g/1½ lb, cut into chunks
garlic cloves	2, crushed
or garlic purée (paste)	10 ml/2 tsp
grated fresh or bottled ginger	15 ml/1 tbsp
ground coriander	15 ml/1 tbsp
cumin seeds	5 ml/1 tsp
ground turmeric	2.5 ml/½ tsp
cayenne pepper	2.5 ml/½ tsp
whole cloves	4
sweet potatoes, peeled and cut into large chunks	450 g/1 lb
can of chopped tomatoes	400 g/14 oz/large
boiling lamb or vegetable stock or water	300 ml/½ pint/1¼ cups
salt and freshly ground black pepper	
plain yoghurt	150 ml/¼ pint/⅔ cup

1 Heat the oil in a large pan and fry the onions for 5 minutes. Add the lamb, garlic, ginger, coriander, cumin seeds, turmeric, cayenne pepper and cloves and cook for 5 minutes, stirring all the time until the lamb is browned all over. Tip the mixture into the ceramic cooking pot.

2 Add the sweet potatoes, tomatoes and stock or water to the pot. Season with salt and pepper, then stir well to mix everything together.

3 Cover with the lid and cook on High for 3 hours or on Low for 6 hours, or until the lamb is very tender. Taste and adjust the seasoning if necessary.

4 Spoon on to warmed plates and drizzle over the yoghurt.

5 Serve with parathas or popadoms.

tip

● Choose a 'sharp' plain yoghurt rather than a mild or creamy variety to help offset the sweetness of this curry.

spiced lamb in almond sauce

Known as badami elachi gosht, this is an elegant and delicate pale-coloured curry, originally created for the Moghul royalty.

SERVES 4
READY IN **4½-6½ HOURS ON LOW**   ②

garlic cloves,	2
or garlic purée (paste)	10 ml/2 tsp
large onion,	1, roughly chopped
or frozen diced onion	60 ml/4 tbsp
green chillies	4, seeded and roughly chopped
light lamb or vegetable stock	250 ml/8 fl oz/1 cup
ground almonds	75 ml/5 tbsp
ghee or unsalted (sweet) butter	30 ml/2 tbsp
green cardamom pods	8, split
ground cinnamon	2.5 ml/½ tsp
lean lamb, cut into chunks	700 g/1½ lb
cornflour (cornstarch)	2.5 ml/½ tsp
thick plain or Greek-style yoghurt	75 ml/5 tbsp
salt and white pepper	
double (heavy) cream	250 ml/8 fl oz/1 cup

1 Put the garlic, onion and chillies in a small food processor and blend until finely chopped. Add 60 ml/ 4 tbsp of the stock and blend to a purée. Mix in the ground almonds.

2 Heat the ghee or butter in a pan, add the purée, cardamom pods and cinnamon and cook for 4–5 minutes, stirring continuously. Stir in the lamb, then turn off the heat. Tip the contents of the pan into the slow cooker, then stir in the rest of the stock. Blend the cornflour with the yoghurt and stir that in too. Season with salt and white pepper.

3 Cover with the lid and cook on Low for 4–6 hours, or until the lamb is fairly tender. Stir in the cream and cook for a further 30 minutes.

4 Taste and adjust the seasoning if necessary.

5 Serve with Saffron Rice (page 143) and Indian chutney.

tip

- You could also serve it with Turmeric Rice (page 143) and an onion salad.

madras lamb curry

One of the most popular restaurant curries, a Madras is named after the city in India now known as Chennai.

SERVES 4
READY IN **6–7 HOURS ON LOW**   ③

groundnut (peanut) or sunflower oil	30 ml/2 tbsp
lean diced lamb	700 g/1½ lb
large onion,	1, chopped
or frozen diced onion	60 ml/ 4 tbsp
Madras curry paste	45–60 ml/3–4 tbsp
very hot (not boiling) vegetable stock	100 ml/3½ fl oz/scant ½ cup
cornflour (cornstarch)	2.5 ml/½ tsp
Greek-style yoghurt	250 ml/8 fl oz/1 cup
salt and freshly ground black pepper	

1 Heat 15 ml/1 tbsp of the oil in a large frying pan. Add the lamb and brown on all sides. Transfer to the ceramic cooking pot with a slotted spoon.

2 Add the remaining 15 ml/1 tbsp of oil to the pan and gently fry the onion for 6–7 minutes, or until almost soft. Stir in the curry paste and cook for another minute. Turn off the heat and stir in about half of the stock. Pour over the lamb.

3 In a separate bowl, blend the cornflour with a spoonful of yoghurt, then stir in the rest of the yoghurt. Stir in the remaining stock, then pour into the ceramic cooking pot. Stir well, then cover with the lid and cook on High for 3 hours or Low for 6–7 hours, or until the lamb is really tender.

4 Taste the sauce and season with salt and pepper if necessary.

5 Serve with chapattis and Cucumber and Coriander Raita (page 158).

tip

- You could serve this with naan breads instead of chapattis.

slow-cooked leg of lamb

If you want to avoid having your oven on for several hours, here's a slow-cooker version of roast lamb, flavoured with spices.

SERVES 4

READY IN **8 HOURS ON LOW** ②

½ leg of lamb	about 900 g/2 lb
groundnut (peanut) or sunflower oil	15ml/1 tbsp
cumin seeds	5 ml/1 tsp
black mustard seeds	5 ml/1 tsp
green cardamom pods	2, seeds reserved and pods discarded
garlic clove,	1, crushed
or garlic purée (paste)	5 ml/1 tsp
grated fresh or bottled ginger	15 ml/1 tbsp
green chilli,	1, seeded and finely chopped
or green chilli purée (paste)	10 ml/2 tsp
paprika	10 ml/2 tsp
thick plain yoghurt	250 ml/8 fl oz/1 cup
soft brown sugar	5 ml/1 tsp
salt	5 ml/1 tsp
hot (not boiling) lamb or vegetable stock or water	60 ml/4 tbsp

1 Make some small shallow slits all over the lamb to allow the flavours to penetrate during cooking.

2 Heat the oil in a small frying pan, add the cumin, mustard and cardamom seeds and cook until they begin to pop. Stir in the garlic, ginger, chilli and paprika and cook for a further minute, stirring. Turn off the heat and leave to cool for a few minutes.

3 Place the yoghurt in a bowl and stir in the spice mixture, sugar and salt. Spread this mixture all over the lamb. Place the lamb in the ceramic cooking pot, then carefully pour in the stock or water between the lamb joint and the side of the pot. Cover with the lid and cook on Low for 8 hours or until the lamb is cooked and very tender.

4 Carefully remove the meat from the slow cooker and carve into thick slices or chunks.

5 Serve with Bombay Potatoes (page 146) and Indian tomato chutney.

tip
● Make sure that the piece of lamb you choose will fit into your slow cooker.

kashmir lamb curry

This recipe demonstrates the diversity of Indian cuisine and is mild yet fragrant. It is typical of the dishes from Kashmir.

SERVES 4
READY IN **4–7 HOURS ON LOW**   ①

lamb shanks	4
salt and freshly ground black pepper	
green cardamom pods	6, split
fennel seeds	5 ml/1 tsp
bay leaves	2
ground ginger	5 ml/1 tsp
ground cinnamon	1.5 ml/¼ tsp
cornflour (cornstarch)	2.5 ml/½ tsp
thick plain yoghurt	300 ml/½ pint/1¼ cups
hot (not boiling) lamb or vegetable stock	250 ml/8 fl oz/1 cup
coriander (cilantro) leaves	a handful, torn into small pieces

1 Remove any excess fat from the lamb shanks. Season well with plenty of salt and pepper. Place in the ceramic cooking pot in a single layer. Add the cardamom pods, fennel seeds and bay leaves.

2 Blend the ginger, cinnamon and cornflour with a little of the yoghurt in a large jug, then stir in the rest of the yoghurt. Gradually stir the stock into the yoghurt and pour over the lamb in the pot.

3 Cover with the lid and cook on Low for 4–7 hours or until the lamb is very tender. Skim any excess fat from the top (alternatively, you can cool the dish, refrigerate overnight and remove the solidified fat before reheating it on the hob).

4 Taste and adjust the seasoning if necessary. Scatter torn coriander leaves over the top.

5 Serve with plain or Lemon-scented Rice (page 143).

tip

- You can brown the lamb shanks first, if you prefer.

pork

Although the Hindus and Muslims of India do not usually eat pork, Indian Christians do, so there are a few pork curries here. Pork is ideal for very spicy dishes. Most curries need a long, slow cooking time so what could be more appropriate than to prepare these wonderful recipes in the slow cooker for the most delicious results?

hot and sour pork curry

The heat of mustard seeds, chilli and ginger and the sharpness of vinegar are mellowed by long slow cooking.

SERVES 4

READY IN **5–7 HOURS ON LOW**

belly of pork	900 g/2 lb, skinned and cut into large cubes
white wine vinegar	90 ml/6 tbsp
hot chilli powder	7.5 ml/1½ tsp
ground turmeric	5 ml/1 tsp
cumin seeds	10 ml/2 tsp
yellow mustard seeds	5 ml/1 tsp
soft dark brown sugar	5 ml/1 tsp
large onion,	1, finely sliced
or frozen diced onion	60 ml/4 tbsp
garlic cloves,	3, crushed
or garlic purée (paste)	15 ml/1 tbsp
grated fresh or bottled ginger	10 ml/2 tsp
salt and freshly ground black pepper	
cold water	350 ml/12 fl oz/1⅓ cups

1 Put the meat in a large non-metallic bowl with the vinegar, chilli powder, turmeric, cumin and mustard seeds and sugar. Mix well, cover and chill for 6 hours, or overnight if preferred.

2 Add the onion, garlic and ginger to the pork. Season well with salt and pepper, then stir everything until thoroughly mixed. Tip into the ceramic cooking pot.

3 Stir in the water, then cover with the lid and cook on Low for 5–7 hours or until the pork is very tender.

4 Skim any fat that is floating on the surface, then taste and adjust the seasoning, if necessary.

5 Serve with Bombay Potatoes (page 146) and Lemon-scented Rice (page 143).

tip
- If possible, make this dish the day before, chill, then skim off the fat before reheating – the flavours will be even better.

goan pork curry

Similar to many pork dishes from Goa, this has a classic tang from the addition of vinegar.

SERVES 4
READY IN **6 HOURS ON LOW**

onions,	2
or frozen diced onion	90 ml/6 tbsp
garlic cloves,	3, crushed
or garlic purée (paste)	15 ml/1 tbsp
grated fresh or bottled ginger	15 ml/1 tbsp
cold water	45 ml/3 tbsp
pork shoulder	700 g/1½ lb, cut into thick strips
groundnut (peanut) or sunflower oil	30 ml/2 tbsp
mustard seeds	5 ml/1 tsp
ground cumin	5 ml/1 tsp
ground cinnamon	2.5 ml/½ tsp
dried chilli flakes	2.5 ml/½ tsp
jaggery or light muscavado sugar	15 ml/1 tbsp
balsamic vinegar	45 ml/3 tbsp
tamarind paste	15 ml/1 tbsp
very hot (not boiling) vegetable stock	400 ml/14 fl oz/1¾ cups
salt	to taste

1 Roughly chop one of the onions (or use half the frozen diced onion) and put in a food processor with the garlic and ginger. Process until finely chopped, then add the cold water and blend to a purée.

2 Pat the pieces of pork dry with kitchen paper (paper towels) to help them brown more efficiently. Heat 15 ml/1 tbsp of the oil in a frying pan over a high heat, add the pork and fry for 3–4 minutes until browned all over. Transfer to the ceramic cooking pot with a slotted spoon.

3 Finely slice the second onion. Heat the remaining 15 ml/1 tbsp of oil and cook the mustard seeds for a few seconds, until fragrant. Add the onion and cook for 7–8 minutes, until beginning to colour. Add the onion purée, cumin, cinnamon, chilli and jaggery and cook for a further 2 minutes, stirring. Stir in the balsamic vinegar, then turn off the heat.

4 In a separate bowl, blend the tamarind paste with a few spoonfuls of the stock, then stir in the rest of it. Pour into the pan, stirring, then tip the mixture over the pork. Stir well, cover with the lid and cook on High for 3 hours or Low for 6 until really tender.

5 Serve spooned over Turmeric Rice (page 143).

pork korma
with spinach

Like most kormas, the sauce is enriched and thickened with almonds, but this version is less rich and doesn't contain cream or ghee.

SERVES 4
READY IN 4¾ HOURS ON LOW

groundnut (peanut) or sunflower oil	15ml/1 tbsp
lean minced (ground) pork	450 g/1 lb
onions,	2, thinly sliced
or frozen diced onion	90 ml/6 tbsp
garlic cloves,	2, crushed
or garlic purée (paste)	10 ml/2 tsp
green cardamom pods	6, seeds reserved and pods discarded
cumin seeds	15 ml/1 tbsp
new potatoes	700 g/1½ lb, scrubbed and halved
hot (not boiling) vegetable or chicken stock	450 ml/¾ pint/2 cups
salt and freshly ground black pepper	
cornflour (cornstarch)	10 ml/2 tsp
thick plain or Greek-style yoghurt	300 ml/½ pint/1¼ cups
ground almonds	75 g/3 oz/¾ cup
baby spinach leaves	150 g/5 oz
flaked (slivered) almonds	25 g/1 oz/¼ cup

1 Heat the oil in a large frying pan over a medium high heat. Add the pork and fry for 2–3 minutes until no longer pink and all the grains are separate. Add the onions, garlic, cardamom seeds and cumin seeds and cook for a further 5 minutes, stirring. Tip the mixture into the ceramic cooking pot.

2 Add the potatoes and stock, season with salt and pepper and mix everything together. Cover with the lid and cook on High for 2 hours or Low for 4 hours.

3 In a separate bowl, blend the cornflour with 150 ml/ ¼ pint/⅔ cup of the yoghurt and the ground almonds. Stir this mixture into the curry. Add the spinach leaves, pressing down into the hot liquid. Cover and cook for a further 30–45 minutes or until the spinach has wilted.

4 Stir the spinach into the curry, taste and adjust the seasoning if necessary. Drizzle with the rest of the yoghurt and sprinkle with the flaked almonds before serving.

5 Serve with warm garlic and coriander naan or chapattis.

variations

- Minced pork has been used in this korma dish, but lean beef or lamb would work equally well.

beef

Because Hindus make up the majority of the Indian population and regard the cow as a sacred animal, beef curries are only served in a few parts of India. Nevertheless, I've included this chapter because the slow cooker excels when it comes to cooking beef, making it succulent and delicious.

Don't go for the most expensive cuts of beef believing that they will produce a better curry. Ideal beef cuts for slow cooking are generally the cheaper ones such as brisket and chuck steak as they have a looser texture. During cooking the fibres open up and allow moisture and spices to penetrate, creating a delicious, rich, tasty sauce.

More expensive cuts, such as fine-grained and densely textured sirloin (porterhouse) steak, are less suitable for slow cooking because the tightness of the fibres prevents them from absorbing the liquid around them. This means that although they become tender when cooked in a slow cooker, the curry will lack succulence and flavour.

beef biryani

In this simplified version of biryani, the meat and rice are cooked separately to allow the beef to benefit from slow cooking.

SERVES 4

READY IN **6-8 HOURS ON LOW**

ghee or unsalted (sweet) butter	30 ml/2 tbsp
onions,	2, thinly sliced
or frozen diced onions	90 ml/6 tbsp
groundnut (peanut) or sunflower oil	15ml/1 tbsp
lean braising or chuck steak	700 g/1½ lb, diced
ground ginger	5 ml/1 tsp
garam masala	5 ml/1 tsp
ground cinnamon	2.5 ml/½ tsp
chilli powder	2.5 ml/½ tsp
caraway seeds	2.5 ml/½ tsp
very hot (not boiling) beef stock	100 ml/3½ fl oz/scant ½ cup
green cardamom pods	2, split
bay leaf	1
thick plain or Greek-style yoghurt	150 ml/¼ pint/⅔ cup
salt and freshly ground black pepper	
basmati rice	350 g/12 oz/1½ cups
frozen peas	75 g/3 oz/½ cup
desiccated (shredded) coconut	45 ml/3 tbsp, to garnish

1 Heat the ghee or butter in a large frying pan. Add the onions and fry, stirring for about 10 minutes, until golden. Transfer to the ceramic cooking pot with a slotted spoon.

2 Heat the oil in the same pan and fry the beef until brown on all sides. Sprinkle over the ginger, garam masala, cinnamon, chilli and caraway seeds. Cook for a further minute. Stir in the beef stock, then tip the mixture into the cooking pot.

3 Add the cardamom pods and bay leaf to the pot, then stir in the yoghurt. Season with salt and pepper, cover with the lid and cook on High for 3–4 hours or Low for 6–8 hours.

4 Meanwhile, cook the rice according to the packet instructions, adding the peas for the last 5 minutes. Drain well.

5 Gently stir the rice into the beef mixture. Spoon on to warmed plates and garnish with the coconut.

6 Serve with popadoms and Sweet Mango Chutney (page 156).

variation

- This biryani can be made with lamb instead of beef, although I suggest you reduce the cooking time by 30 minutes if cooking on High, 1 hour on Low.

bangladeshi beef curry

Known as rezala, a small amount of stock and yoghurt sauce just coats the beef, so serve this dish with moist accompaniment.

SERVES 4
READY IN 6–8 HOURS ON LOW ②

ghee or unsalted (sweet) butter	60 ml/4 tbsp
braising or chuck steak	700 g/1½ lb, cut into 4 cm/1½ in cubes
onions,	2, sliced
or frozen diced onions	90 ml/6 tbsp
garlic clove,	1, crushed
or garlic purée (paste)	5 ml/1 tsp
green chilli	1, seeded and finely chopped
or green chilli paste	5 ml/1 tsp
green cardamom pods	4, split
whole cloves	4
ground cumin	5 ml/1 tsp
ground coriander	5 ml/1 tsp
ground turmeric	5 ml/1 tsp
cayenne pepper	2.5 ml/½ tsp
caster (superfine) sugar	2.5 ml/½ tsp
salt	2.5 ml/½ tsp
beef stock or water	100 ml/3½ fl oz/scant ½ cup
thick plain yoghurt	300 ml/½ pint/1¼ cups

1 Heat half the ghee or butter in a large frying pan and cook the beef in batches until browned all over. Transfer to the ceramic cooking pot with a slotted spoon, leaving the fat and juices behind.

2 Add the rest of the ghee or butter to the pan and cook the onions for 7–8 minutes until they begin to colour. Add the garlic, chilli, cardamom pods, cloves, cumin, coriander, turmeric, cayenne pepper and sugar and stir for a further 1–2 minutes. Stir in the salt and stock or water. Turn off the heat and tip the mixture into the ceramic cooking pot.

3 Stir the yoghurt into the curry a little at a time. Cover with the lid and cook on High for 3–4 hours or on Low for 6–8 hours, or until the meat is really tender and the sauce very thick.

4 Taste and adjust the seasoning if necessary.

5 Serve with basmati rice and a lentil dish.

tip

- You could use vegetable stock if you prefer. Although Bangladesh is not in India, we thought this was a lovely curry.

beef keema

Make sure you use good quality lean mince for this mild curry. It's delicious served with freshly cooked parathas or chapattis.

SERVES 4

READY IN **4¼ HOURS ON LOW**

groundnut (peanut) or sunflower oil	30 ml/2 tbsp
large onion,	1, finely chopped
or frozen diced onions	60 ml/4 tbsp
garlic cloves	2, crushed
or garlic purée (paste)	10 ml/2 tsp
1 green chilli (optional),	1, seeded and finely chopped
or green chilli purée (paste) (optional)	5 ml/1 tsp
grated fresh or bottled ginger	5 ml/1 tsp
mild curry paste	15 ml/1 tbsp
lean minced (ground) beef	450 g/1 lb
caster (superfine) sugar	2.5 ml/½ tsp
tomato purée (paste)	30 ml/2 tbsp
boiling beef stock or water	150 ml/¼ pint/⅔ cup
can of chopped tomatoes	400 g/14 oz/large
salt and freshly ground black pepper	
fresh or frozen peas	175 g/6 oz/1 cup

1 Heat the oil in a large frying pan and fry the onion for 7–8 minutes, until almost soft. Add the garlic, chilli, if using, ginger and curry paste and stir for a few seconds until mixed.

2 Add the minced beef and stir-fry for 3–4 minutes until the meat is no longer pink and all the grains are separate. Stir in the sugar, tomato purée and about half the stock or water. Heat until steaming hot, but not boiling.

3 Tip the mixture into the ceramic cooking pot, stir in the rest of the stock or water and chopped tomatoes. Season with salt and pepper, then cover with the lid and cook on High for 2 hours or on Low for 4 hours or until the meat is tender and the sauce thick.

4 If using frozen peas, spread them out on a plate to thaw while the meat is cooking. Put the peas in a sieve (strainer) and pour over about half a kettleful of boiling water, so that the peas are hot when added to the cooking pot. Stir the peas into the minced beef mixture, put the lid back on and cook for a further 15 minutes. Taste and adjust the seasoning if necessary.

5 Serve with Indian breads.

variation

- This keema is equally good made with lamb instead of beef; the cooking times remain the same.

madras beef curry

A rich and satisfying dish with aromatic-flavoured meat that has been cooked for so long, it almost melts in your mouth.

SERVES 4

READY IN 6-8 HOURS ON LOW

green cardamom pods	2, split
coriander seeds	5 ml/1 tsp
cumin seeds	5 ml/1 tsp
crushed dried chillies	5 ml/1 tsp
black peppercorns	5
salt	2.5 ml/½ tsp
grated fresh or bottled ginger	10 ml/2 tsp
onions,	2
or frozen diced onions	90 ml/6 tbsp
garlic cloves,	2, crushed
or garlic purée (paste)	10 ml/2 tsp
tomato purée (paste)	15 ml/1 tbsp
braising or chuck steak	700 g/1½ lb, cut into cubes
ghee or unsalted (sweet) butter	30 ml/2 tbsp
groundnut (peanut) or sunflower oil	15ml/1 tbsp
hot beef stock	100 ml/3½ fl oz/scant ½ cup
cornflour (cornstarch)	2.5 ml/½ tsp
thick plain yoghurt	250 ml/8 fl oz/1 cup

1 Open the cardamom pods and remove the black seeds. Put them into a spice or coffee grinder with the coriander and cumin seeds, chillies, peppercorns and salt. Grind to a coarse powder. Add the ginger, one of the onions, roughly chopped, the garlic and tomato purée. Blend to a fairly smooth paste.

2 Put the beef in a glass bowl. Add the curry paste and mix well until the meat is coated. Tightly cover with clingfilm (plastic wrap) and leave to marinate in the fridge for at least 1 hour, or overnight, if you prefer.

3 Thinly slice the remaining onion. Heat half the ghee or butter with 5 ml/1 tsp of the oil in a large frying pan and cook the onion for 6–7 minutes or until beginning to turn golden. Transfer to the ceramic pot. Add the rest of the ghee or butter and oil to the pan, then cook the beef for 3–4 minutes until browned all over. Turn off the heat and stir in the stock. Tip the mixture into the ceramic cooking pot.

4 In a separate bowl, blend the cornflour with a spoonful of yoghurt, then mix with the rest of the yoghurt. Gradually stir into the beef mixture. Cover with the lid and cook on High for 3–4 hours or on Low for 6–8 hours, until the beef is really tender.

5 Serve with Indian breads such as naan or parathas.

tip

• Although not so authentic, you can save time by buying Madras curry paste, blending 45 ml/3 tbsp with 15 ml/ 1 tbsp water and adding it at step 2.

beef pathia

Also known as patia, this version is less bright than those served in Indian restaurants where red food dye is added.

SERVES 4

READY IN **6-8 HOURS ON LOW**   ②

groundnut (peanut) or sunflower oil	15ml/1 tbsp
ghee or unsalted (sweet) butter	30 ml/2 tbsp
lean braising or chuck steak	700 g/1½ lb, diced
cumin seeds	5 ml/1 tsp
large onion,	1, chopped
or frozen diced onion	60 ml/2 tbsp
garlic cloves,	2, crushed
or garlic purée (paste)	10 ml/2 tsp
grated fresh or bottled ginger	10 ml/2 tsp
medium or hot curry powder	15 ml/1 tbsp
hot chilli powder	5 ml/1 tsp
ground turmeric	10 ml/2 tsp
garam masala	10 ml/2 tsp
ground cinnamon	a pinch
tomato purée (paste)	30 ml/2 tbsp
tamarind purée (paste)	15 ml/1 tbsp
very hot (not boiling) beef stock	300 ml/½ pint/1¼ cups
can of chopped tomatoes	400 g/14 oz/large
salt	to taste

1 Heat the oil and half of the ghee or butter in a large frying pan. Add the beef and fry until browned on all sides. Transfer to the ceramic cooking pot with a slotted spoon, leaving the fat and any juices behind.

2 Add the cumin seeds to the pan and cook for a few seconds until they start to sizzle. Add the rest of the ghee or butter and the onion and cook for 6–7 minutes until beginning to soften.

3 Add the garlic, ginger, curry powder, chilli powder, turmeric, garam masala and cinnamon. Cook for a further minute, stirring. Turn off the heat.

4 In a bowl, blend the tomato and tamarind purées with a few spoonfuls of the stock, then stir in the rest of the stock. Add to the frying pan, stir, then tip the mixture over the beef. Add the chopped tomatoes and season with a little salt.

5 Stir, then cover with the lid and cook on Low for 6–8 hours or until the beef is very tender.

6 Serve with rice and peas.

tip

- You can make this curry milder by reducing the strength of curry and chilli powders.

beef in spiced yoghurt

Cooking in a slow cooker covered with a tea towel echoes the cooking method known as 'dum' in which a paste seals the pot.

SERVES 4
READY IN **5–8 HOURS ON LOW**   ①

groundnut (peanut) or sunflower oil	45 ml/3 tbsp
lean braising or chuck steak	700 g/1½ lb, diced
large onion,	1, chopped
or frozen chopped onion	60 ml/4 tbsp
garlic cloves,	4, crushed
or garlic purée (paste)	20 ml/4 tsp
paprika	15 ml/1 tbsp
ground ginger	5 ml/1 tsp
cayenne pepper	1.5 ml/¼ tsp
strong beef stock	100 ml/3½ fl oz/scant ½ cup
salt and freshly ground black pepper	
cornflour (cornstarch)	2.5 ml/½ tsp
thick plain or Greek-style yoghurt	300 ml/½ pint/1¼ cups

1 Heat 15 ml/1 tbsp of the oil in a large frying pan and fry the beef until it is browned all over. Transfer to the ceramic cooking pot with a slotted spoon.

2 Add the remaining 30 ml/2 tbsp oil to the pan. Fry the onion, stirring continuously, for 6–7 minutes, until almost soft. Stir in the garlic, paprika, ginger and cayenne pepper and cook for a further 30 seconds. Turn off the heat and stir in the stock.

3 Season with salt and pepper, then pour the mixture over the beef. In a separate bowl, blend the cornflour with a spoonful of the yoghurt, then add the rest of the yoghurt. Stir into the beef mixture.

4 Cover with the lid, then place a folded tea towel over the lid and cook on Low for 5–8 hours or until the beef is very tender.

5 Serve with Coconut or Saffron Rice (page 143) or Mushroom Pilau (page 144).

tip

- The steak should be lean but it is not necessary to use an expensive cut.

beef pasanda

For a less rich dish, use Greek-style yoghurt instead of the cream. Serve with lemon-scented rice and mango chutney.

SERVES 4
READY IN **6-8 HOURS ON LOW**   ②

unsalted cashew nuts	50 g/2 oz/½ cup
blanched almonds	50 g/2 oz/½ cup
sesame seeds	15 ml/1 tbsp
grated fresh or bottled ginger	15 ml/1 tbsp
garlic cloves	2
cold water	30 ml/2 tbsp
groundnut (peanut) or sunflower oil	30 ml/2 tbsp
lean braising or chuck steak	700 g/1½ lb, cut into 4 cm/1½ in chunks
large onion,	1, chopped
or frozen diced onion	60 ml/2 tbsp
ground coriander	10 ml/2 tsp
ground cumin	10 ml/2 tsp
ground turmeric	5 ml/1 tsp
green cardamom pods	6, split
whole cloves	4
very hot (not boiling) beef stock	150 ml/¼ pint/⅔ cup
coconut milk	150 ml/¼ pint/⅔ cup
double (heavy) cream	150 ml/¼ pint/⅔ cup
fresh or bottled lemon juice	15 ml/1 tbsp
salt	to taste

1 Put the cashews and almonds in a non-stick frying pan over a low heat and cook, stirring frequently for 2 minutes. Add the sesame seeds and continue cooking until just starting to turn golden brown. Remove from the heat and leave to cool.

2 Tip the nuts and seeds into a spice or coffee grinder and process until the nuts are finely chopped. Blend with the ginger, garlic and cold water to make a smooth purée.

3 Heat 15 ml/1 tbsp of oil in the pan and fry the beef until browned all over. Transfer to the ceramic cooking pot using a slotted spoon, leaving the fat and juices behind in the pan.

4 Add the remaining 15 ml/1 tbsp oil to the pan and cook the onion for 5 minutes. Stir in the ground coriander, cumin, turmeric, cardamom pods and cloves, followed by the nut purée. Cook, stirring, for 2 minutes. Stir in the stock.

5 Tip the mixture over the beef, then stir in the coconut milk and cream. Cover with the lid and cook on Low for 6–8 hours, or until the beef is very tender.

6 Stir in the lemon juice and salt to taste.

7 Serve with Lemon-scented Rice (page 143) and Indian chutney.

variation

- This pasanda is equally good made with lamb or chicken thighs cooked on Low for 5–7 hours.

royal beef with almond sauce

Simple accompaniments such as steamed basmati rice and warm naan bread are all that is needed to serve with this curry.

SERVES 4
READY IN **6-8 HOURS ON LOW**   ①

garlic cloves, crushed, or garlic purée (paste)	4 20 ml/4 tsp
grated fresh or bottled ginger	15 ml/1 tbsp
blanched almonds	50 g/2 oz/½ cup
cold water	60 ml/4 tbsp
groundnut (peanut) or sunflower oil	30 ml/2 tbsp
beef, braising or chuck steak	700 g/1½ lb, cubed
large onion, or frozen diced onion	1, chopped 60 ml/2 tbsp
green cardamom pods	6, split
whole cloves	6
ground cinnamon	1.5 ml/¼ tsp
ground coriander	5 ml/1 tsp
ground cumin	10 ml/2 tsp
cayenne pepper	a pinch
very hot (not boiling) light beef or vegetable stock	350 ml/12 fl oz/1⅓ cups
double (heavy) cream	150 ml/¼ pint/⅔ cup
salt and freshly ground black pepper	
garam masala	5 ml/1 tsp

1 Put the garlic, ginger and almonds in a spice or coffee grinder or small food processor and blend until finely chopped. Add the water and blend to a smooth purée.

2 Heat 15 ml/1 tbsp of the oil in a large frying pan and fry the beef until browned all over. Transfer to the ceramic cooking pot with a slotted spoon.

3 Add the remaining oil to the pan and fry the onion for 6–7 minutes until almost soft. Stir in the cardamom pods, cloves, cinnamon, coriander, cumin and cayenne pepper and the almond purée. Cook, stirring, for a further 2 minutes.

4 Turn off the heat and stir in the stock and cream. Season with salt and pepper and tip the mixture over the beef in the pot. Stir well.

5 Cover with the lid and cook on Low for 6–8 hours or until the beef is very tender. Stir in the garam masala, then taste and adjust the seasoning if necessary.

6 Serve with basmati rice or naan bread and a salad.

tip

• The whole spices aren't meant to be eaten, so remove them, if you prefer, before serving.

beef bhuna

Bhuna is the term of the technique in which spices are cooked in oil to bring out their flavour. This version uses bhuna curry paste.

SERVES 4
READY IN **5–8 HOURS ON LOW** ②

groundnut (peanut) or sunflower oil	30 ml/2 tbsp
onion,	1, chopped
or frozen diced onion	45 ml/3 tbsp
bhuna curry paste	75 ml/5 tbsp
braising or chuck steak	700 g/1½ lb, cubed
can of chopped tomatoes	200 g/7 oz/small
boiling beef stock	120 ml/4 fl oz/½ cup
salt	to taste

1 Heat the oil in a large non-stick frying pan, add the onion and cook, stirring frequently, for 5 minutes. Stir in the curry paste and cook for about 15 seconds more.

2 Add the beef and continue cooking over a medium heat for a further 3–4 minutes, stirring until the spices are very fragrant and the beef is beginning to brown.

3 Tip the mixture into the pot, then stir in the tomatoes and stock. Cover with the lid and cook on Low for 5–8 hours, or until the beef is very tender. Taste and season with salt if necessary.

4 Serve with Carrot and Coriander Raita (page 158) and warmed Indian breads.

fish and seafood

Much of India is surrounded by sea, abundant with fish and seafood, and this is reflected in its range of wonderful curries. Healthy and delicious, fish is eminently suitable for the slow cooker as the gentle, even cooking ensures that it retains its shape and texture during cooking.

Although large whole fish won't fit into the slow cooker, it's absolutely perfect for fish steaks and fillets. Unlike meat, fish cooks relatively quickly in the slow cooker so is unsuitable for all-day cooking and you will find that many of the dishes in this chapter cook in less than 2 hours.

When buying fish and seafood, remember that if it's really fresh it shouldn't smell too 'fishy'. Obviously, it's difficult to test pre-packed fish for freshness, but buy from a reliable source and make sure that it looks firm and moist.

Both fresh and frozen seafood should be put in the refrigerator or freezer as soon as possible and, ideally, fresh fish should be cooked and eaten on the day you buy it.

keralan fish curry

There is no need to marinate the fish as the aromatic flavours will seep into it. Serve with rice to soak up the sauce.

SERVES 4
READY IN 1¼-1½ HOURS ON LOW ①

ground turmeric	2.5 ml/½ tsp
paprika	10 ml/2 tsp
lime juice	from 1 lime
firm white fish such as turbot	450 g/1 lb, cut into large bite-sized chunks
mustard seeds	5 ml/1 tsp
fenugreek seeds	1.5 ml/¼ tsp
sunflower oil	15 ml/1 tbsp
onion,	1, chopped
or frozen diced onion	45 ml/3 tbsp
garlic cloves,	2, crushed
or garlic purée (paste)	10 ml/2 tsp
grated fresh or bottled ginger	15 ml/1 tbsp
crushed dried red chillies	1.5 ml/¼ tsp
ground coriander	5 ml/1 tsp
coconut milk	250 ml/8 fl oz/1 cup
salt and freshly ground black pepper	

1 Mix the turmeric, paprika and lime juice in the ceramic cooking pot. Add the chunks of fish and stir to coat. Leave to marinade for a few minutes.

2 Meanwhile, put the mustard and fenugreek seeds in a dry non-stick frying pan over a medium heat for 1–2 minutes until they give off a spicy aroma. Tip on to a small bowl or plate.

3 Add the oil to the pan and fry the onion for 7–8 minutes until soft. Add the garlic, ginger, chillies, ground coriander and mustard and fenugreek seeds. Cook for 1 more minute, stirring all the time. Turn off the heat, then stir in the coconut milk and season with salt and pepper.

4 Pour the spicy coconut mixture over the fish and stir well. Cover with the lid and switch the slow cooker on to Low. Cook for 1¼–1½ hours or until the fish is cooked and opaque.

5 Serve with rice and wedges of fresh lime, if you like.

tip
• Remember that fish cooks quickly so cannot be left for too long before serving, even in the slow cooker.

creamy coconut salmon

Salmon is quite a firm fish and retains its shape and texture well in the slow cooker. Here it's cooked in a mildly spiced sauce.

SERVES 4

READY IN **3 HOURS ON LOW** ①

sunflower oil	15 ml/1 tbsp
onion,	1, finely chopped
or frozen diced onion	45 ml/3 tbsp
garlic cloves,	2, crushed
or garlic purée (paste)	10 ml/2 tsp
grated fresh or bottled ginger	10 ml/2 tsp
fresh green chilli,	1, seeded and chopped
or green chilli purée (paste)	5 ml/1 tsp
ground cumin	5 ml/1 tsp
ground coriander	5 ml/1 tsp
chilli powder	5 ml/1 tsp
ground turmeric	2.5 ml/½ tsp
lemon juice	15 ml/1 tbsp
coconut milk	250 ml/8 fl oz/1 cup
salmon steaks	4, each about 175 g/6 oz
salt and freshly ground black pepper	

1 Heat the oil in a frying pan, add the onion and gently fry for 5 minutes, stirring often. Add the garlic, ginger, chilli, cumin, coriander, chilli powder and turmeric and cook for a further 2 minutes, stirring all the time. Turn off the heat and stir in the lemon juice.

2 Spoon the mixture into a food processor or blender and pour in about half of the coconut milk. Blend to a smooth purée.

3 Tip the purée into the ceramic cooking pot and stir in the rest of the coconut milk. Cover with the lid and switch on the slow cooker. Cook for 1 hour on High or 2 hours on Low.

4 Add the salmon steaks to the sauce, arranging them in a single layer and spooning some of the sauce over the top to keep the fish moist as it cooks. Cover with the lid again and cook on Low for a further 45–60 minutes or until the fish flakes easily and is tender.

5 Lift the fish on to warmed serving plates and spoon the sauce over.

6 Serve with basmati rice and Cucumber and Coriander Raita (page 158).

variation

- Use any firm-fleshed fish instead of salmon.

mackerel curry with coconut

The robust texture of mackerel makes it ideal for curries. Because it is a strongly flavoured fish, it isn't overpowered.

SERVES 4
READY IN **2 HOURS ON LOW**   ②

whole mackerel	about 550 g/1¼ lb, cleaned and cut into steaks 4 cm/1½ in thick
curry leaves	6
green chillies	3, left whole
groundnut (peanut) or sunflower oil	30 ml/2 tbsp
large onion,	1, chopped
or frozen diced onion	60 ml/ 4 tbsp
garlic cloves,	2, crushed
or garlic purée (paste)	10 ml/2 tsp
grated fresh or bottled ginger	15 ml/1 tbsp
fenugreek	2.5 ml/½ tsp
cumin seeds	5 ml/1 tsp
ground turmeric	5 ml/1 tsp
chilli powder	5 ml/1 tsp
ground coriander	10 ml/2 tsp
tamarind paste	5 ml/1 tsp
hot vegetable stock	150 ml/¼ pint/⅔ cup
coconut milk	250 ml/8 fl oz/1 cup
salt	to taste

1 Rinse the mackerel steaks under cold running water and place in a single layer in the ceramic cooking pot. Add the curry leaves and whole green chillies.

2 Heat the oil in a frying pan and fry the onion for 6–7 minutes or until almost soft. Stir in the garlic, ginger, fenugreek and cumin seeds, turmeric, chilli powder and ground coriander and cook for a further 2 minutes, stirring all the time. Turn off the heat.

3 In a bowl, blend the tamarind with a few spoonfuls of stock, then stir in the rest of the stock. Add to the pan with the coconut milk and season with a little salt. Pour over the fish.

4 Cover with the lid and switch on the slow cooker. Cook for 1 hour on High or for 2 hours on Low, or until the mackerel is opaque and flakes easily from the bone.

5 Serve with plain boiled basmati rice.

tip

- Buy large mackerel for this recipe and cut it across into thick steaks (or ask the fishmonger to do this for you); cooking the fish on the bone adds to the flavour of the sauce.

mangalorean fish curry

This unusual curry comes from the south west coast of India, abundant in fish and seafood. It is served with tiny dumplings.

SERVES 4
READY IN **1 HOUR ON LOW**   ②

onion,	1, roughly chopped
or frozen diced onions	60 ml/4 tbsp
garlic cloves,	3, peeled
or garlic purée (paste)	15 ml/1 tbsp
creamed coconut	100 g/4 oz, roughly chopped
cumin seeds	5 ml/1 tsp
coriander seeds	10 ml/2 tsp
mustard seeds	2.5 ml/½ tsp
ground turmeric	2.5 ml/½ tsp
chilli powder	2.5 ml/½ tsp
hot (not boiling) fish or vegetable stock	600 ml/1 pint/2½ cups
groundnut (peanut) or sunflower oil	15 ml/1 tbsp
tamarind paste	5 ml/1 tsp
firm white fish, skinned	700–900 g/1½–2lb
salt and freshly ground black pepper	
For the dumplings:	
rice flour	100 g/4 oz/1 cup
salt	2.5 ml/½ tsp
cold water	90 ml/6 tbsp

1 Put the onion, garlic, 75 g/3 oz of the creamed coconut, cumin, coriander and mustard seeds, turmeric and chilli powder in a food processor or blender with a few tablespoons of the fish or vegetable stock. Process until finely chopped. Add a further 150ml/¼ pint/⅔ cup of the stock and blend until smooth.

2 Heat the oil in a frying pan and pour in the purée. Cook until all the liquid has evaporated and the spices have reduced to a thick paste. Turn off the heat. Add the tamarind paste then gradually stir in the rest of the stock. Pour into the ceramic cooking pot, cover with the lid and switch on to High. Leave to cook for a few minutes while preparing the fish and dumplings.

3 Cut the fish into 4 cm/1½ in chunks and lightly season with salt and pepper.

4 For the dumplings, sift the flour and a pinch of salt into a bowl. Finely grate the remaining 25 g/1 oz creamed coconut and stir into the flour. Stir in the cold water and mix to a soft dough. Shape into 16 small balls.

5 Stir the fish into the curry sauce. Add the dumplings in a single layer on top, spacing them slightly apart. Put the lid back on, switch on to Low and cook for about 1 hour or until both the fish and dumplings are cooked. Taste and adjust the seasoning, if necessary.

6 Serve with steamed green beans or spinach.

tip

- Always use floured hands when shaping dumplings and don't knead them for any longer than necessary.

goan prawn curry

This curry is really quick and simple to make, especially if you use ready-prepared prawns. Pat them dry on kitchen paper.

SERVES 4

READY IN **3¼–5½ HOURS ON LOW**   ①

ground coriander	30 ml/2 tbsp
paprika	15 ml/1 tbsp
ground cumin	5 ml/1 tsp
cayenne pepper	2.5 ml/½ tsp
ground turmeric	1.5 ml/¼ tsp
salt and freshly ground black pepper	
lemon juice	15 ml/1 tbsp
water	100 ml/3¼ fl oz/scant ½ cup
large shallots,	2, finely chopped
or frozen chopped shallots	30 ml/2 tbsp
can of coconut milk	400 ml/14 fl oz/large
raw prawns (shrimp)	400 g/14 oz large, peeled and de-veined
chopped fresh or thawed frozen coriander (cilantro)	45 ml/3 tbsp

1 Put the ground coriander, paprika, cumin, cayenne pepper, turmeric, salt and pepper into the ceramic cooking pot. Add the lemon juice, then gradually blend in the water to make a smooth paste.

2 Stir in the shallots and coconut milk. Cover with the lid and switch the slow cooker on to Low. Cook for 3–5 hours or until the shallots are very tender.

3 Stir the prawns into the sauce, replace the cover and cook for a further 15–30 minutes or until the prawns are just cooked and have turned completely pink and opaque.

4 Stir in the chopped coriander. Taste and adjust the seasoning if necessary.

5 Serve the prawns and sauce on a bed of steamed or boiled basmati rice.

variation

- You can use this basic sauce to make a Goan fish curry, by replacing the prawns with an equal weight of firm white fish, such as haddock, removing the skin and any bones and cutting it into 4 cm/1½ in chunks.

coconut jinga

This is an easy version using spring onions, which don't need pre-cooking, bought curry paste and cooked prawns.

SERVES 4
READY IN 2¼-3¼ HOURS ON LOW ①

spring onions (scallions)	1 bunch
fresh or bottled lemon or lime juice	10 ml/2 tsp
grated fresh or bottled ginger	5 ml/1 tsp
mild or medium curry paste, such korma or tikka	30 ml/2 tbsp
creamed coconut	75 g/3 oz, roughly chopped
tomato purée (paste)	5 ml/1 tsp
very hot (not boiling) vegetable stock or water	150 ml/¼ pint/⅔ cup
cooked shelled prawns (shrimp)	450 g/1 lb
chopped fresh or frozen coriander (cilantro)	30 ml/2 tbsp
salt and freshly ground black pepper	
flaked or desiccated (dried) coconut	

1 Trim the roots and most of the dark green stalks off the spring onions and finely slice them. Put in the ceramic cooking pot and switch the slow cooker on to High or Auto.

2 In a bowl, stir the citrus juice, ginger, curry paste, creamed coconut and tomato purée into the vegetable stock or water until the coconut has dissolved. Pour this over the spring onions. Cover with the lid and cook on High or Auto for 1–1½ hours, or switch to Low and cook for 2–3 hours, until the spring onions are tender.

3 Drain the prawns in a sieve (strainer), then stir into the hot sauce. Replace the cover and cook for a further 15 minutes or until heated through.

4 Stir in the chopped coriander and season with salt and pepper. Sprinkle with some flaked or desiccated coconut.

5 Serve with basmati rice.

tips

- For the garnish, you can lightly toast the desiccated coconut by dry-frying it in a non-stick pan over a medium heat for 2–3 minutes, stirring all the time.

- This dish also makes a fabulous topping for baked potatoes.

kerala prawn curry

Used extensively in Indian cooking, tamarind comes from the seed pods harvested from tamarind trees.

SERVES 4
READY IN 2½ HOURS ON LOW ②

tamarind paste	5 ml/1 tsp
ground cumin	5 ml/1 tsp
ground turmeric	5 ml/1 tsp
boiling vegetable stock or water	120 ml/4 fl oz/½ cup
garlic cloves,	2, finely chopped
or garlic purée (paste)	10 ml/2 tsp
grated fresh or bottled ginger	5 ml/1 tsp
red chilli,	1, seeded and finely chopped
or chilli paste	5 ml/1 tsp
coconut milk	150 ml/¼ pint/⅔ cup
large raw prawns (shrimp)	400 g/14 oz, peeled and de-veined
chopped fresh or frozen coriander (cilantro)	30 ml/2 tbsp
salt and freshly ground black pepper	

1 Put the tamarind paste, cumin and turmeric in a small bowl. Add 60 ml/4 tbsp of the boiling stock or water and stir until blended.

2 Put the garlic, ginger, chilli and coconut milk in the ceramic cooking pot. Stir in the tamarind mixture and the rest of the stock or water. Cover with the lid and cook on High for 1 hour or on Low for 2 hours.

3 Stir in the prawns. Cook for a further 15 minutes on High or 30 minutes on Low or until the prawns turn pink and are just cooked through.

4 Stir in the chopped coriander, taste and season with salt and pepper.

5 Serve with basmati rice and with wedges of lime to squeeze over the prawns, if you like.

tip

- Tamarind paste is easy to buy in Asian grocery stores or major supermarkets.

king prawn and spinach balti

The term 'balti' refers to the steel or iron cooking pot in which the food is cooked, but a slow cooker works just as well.

SERVES 4
READY IN 2¼-3¼ HOURS ON LOW ②

creamed coconut	100 g/4 oz, chopped
hot (not boiling) vegetable stock	450 ml/¾ pint/2 cups
balti curry paste	45 ml/3 tbsp
garlic cloves,	2, crushed
or garlic purée (paste)	10 ml/2 tsp
red chilli (optional),	1, seeded and finely chopped
or red chilli purée (paste) (optional)	5 ml/1 tsp
onion,	1, finely chopped
or frozen diced onion	45 ml/3 tbsp
roughly chopped fresh or frozen cooked spinach	100 g/4 oz
peeled raw tiger prawns (jumbo shrimp)	400 g/14 oz
chopped fresh or thawed frozen coriander (cilantro)	60 ml/4 tbsp
salt and freshly ground black pepper	

1 Put the creamed coconut in the ceramic cooking pot. Add the stock and stir until the coconut has dissolved.

2 Stir in the curry paste, garlic and chilli (if using) until blended. Add the onion, cover with the lid and switch on the slow cooker to Low. Cook for 2–3 hours or until the onion is very tender.

3 Meanwhile, if you are using frozen spinach, put it in a sieve (strainer) over a bowl and leave to defrost and drain at room temperature. Stir the thawed or fresh spinach into the curry mixture along with the prawns and most of the chopped coriander. Cook for a further 15 minutes or until the prawns are tender and completely pink.

4 Taste and season with salt and pepper.

5 Serve with the remaining coriander sprinkled over and warm naan bread.

tip

• Balti is traditionally served without a knife and fork; torn pieces of warmed naan bread are used to scoop up the curry.

vegetable and vegetarian

Indian vegetarian cuisine is incredibly varied and you'll find a great choice of mouth-watering curries in this chapter. Many are based on vegetables, others on beans and pulses and a few on eggs or paneer – a delicious fresh Indian cheese.

You don't have to be a vegetarian to enjoy these meat-free and fish-free dishes.

Because food gently simmers rather than boils in the slow cooker, vegetables retain their shape and texture and are complemented by the use of spices. Slow cooking also ensures that you retain most of their nutrients, as the cooking juices become part of the curry sauce.

vegetable kashmiri

Vary the vegetables according to your personal taste and seasonal availability. This is delicious served with parathas or pooris.

SERVES 4

READY IN 5–6 HOURS ON LOW

green cardamom pods discarded	2, seeds removed and pods
cumin seeds	10 ml/2 tsp
black peppercorns	4
ground cinnamon	2.5 ml/½ tsp
freshly ground nutmeg	2.5 ml/½ tsp
chilli powder	2.5 ml/½ tsp
salt	2.5 ml/½ tsp
groundnut (peanut) or sunflower oil	45 ml/3 tbsp
green chilli,	1, seeded and finely chopped
or green chilli purée (paste)	10 ml/2 tsp
grated fresh or bottled ginger	15 ml/1 tbsp
large potatoes	2, peeled and cut into 2.5 cm/1 in chunks
cauliflower	½, broken into smaller florets
hot (not boiling) vegetable stock	450 ml/¾ pint/2 cups
Greek-style yoghurt	150 ml/1¼ pint/⅔ cup
okra	225 g/8 oz, thickly sliced
flaked (slivered) almonds	50 g/2 oz/½ cup, toasted

1 Put the cardamom seeds, cumin seeds and peppercorns in a mortar or spice grinder and grind until fairly fine. Mix together with the cinnamon, nutmeg, chilli powder and salt.

2 Heat the oil in a frying pan, add the green chilli and ginger and fry for 1 minute, stirring continuously. Add the ground spice mixture and continue frying for a further 2 minutes, stirring to prevent the spices sticking. Turn off the heat.

3 Put the potatoes and cauliflower in the ceramic cooking pot. Stir a little of the stock into the spice mixture, then tip over the vegetables. Stir to coat them evenly in the mixture. Pour in the rest of the stock, cover the slow cooker with a lid and switch on to Low. Cook for 3 hours.

4 Stir a few spoonfuls of the stock from the slow cooker into the yoghurt in a bowl. Add the okra and the yoghurt to the pot and stir until combined.

5 Cook for a further 2–3 hours or until all the vegetables are very tender. Sprinkle with toasted flaked almonds.

6 Serve with Indian breads such as parathas or pooris.

tip

- Use ¼ tsp of ground cardamom if you don't have the pods.

potato and chick pea curry

'Aloo chana' comes from the Punjab, a northern state in India. The slow cooker is brilliant for cooking pulses.

SERVES 4
READY IN **10–12 HOURS ON LOW**   ②

dried chick peas (garbanzos)	225 g/8 oz/1½ cups
bay leaf	1
groundnut (peanut) or sunflower oil	30 ml/2 tbsp
large onion,	1, chopped
or frozen diced onions	60 ml/ 4 tbsp
garlic clove,	1, crushed
or garlic purée (paste)	5 ml/1 tsp
grated fresh or bottled ginger	15 ml/1 tbsp
ground cumin	5 ml/1 tsp
ground coriander	5 ml/1 tsp
green cardamom pods	2, split
green chilli,	1, seeded and finely chopped
or green chilli purée (paste)	5 ml/1 tsp
vegetable stock or water	150 ml/¼ pint/⅔ cups
large potatoes	2, peeled and cut into 2.5 cm/1 in chunks
salt and freshly ground black pepper	

1 Put the chick peas in a large bowl and cover with plenty of cold water. Leave to soak for at least 6 hours, or overnight, if preferred.

2 Drain the soaked chick peas and tip into a saucepan. Pour over just enough boiling water to cover and add the bay leaf. Bring to the boil and boil rapidly for 10 minutes. Turn off the heat and leave to cool for 3–5 minutes, then tip the chick peas with the cooking water into the ceramic cooking pot. Cover with the lid and cook on High for 3–4 hours or Low for 6–8 hours, until tender and most of the liquid has been absorbed.

3 Meanwhile, heat the oil in a frying pan and cook the onion for 10 minutes until beginning to turn golden, stirring frequently. Stir in the garlic, ginger, cumin, ground coriander, cardamom pods and chilli. Cook for 1 more minute. Turn off the heat and stir in the stock or water.

4 Add the potatoes to the chick peas and season with salt and pepper. Pour the onion and spice mixture on top and stir well. Replace the lid and cook on High for a further 2 hours or on Low for 4 hours, until tender. Taste and adjust the seasoning if necessary.

5 Serve with warmed Indian breads.

tip

- If you haven't time to soak and pre-cook dried chick peas, use two large cans of chick peas, drained and rinsed, instead with 60 ml/4 tbsp extra stock or water and start from step 3.

vegetable curry

A satisfying main course with loads of flavour: aubergine, red pepper, carrot, potato and broccoli.

SERVES 4
READY IN 6 HOURS ON LOW   ②

ghee or unsalted (sweet) butter	30 ml/2 tbsp
large onion	1, chopped
or frozen diced onion	60 ml/2 tbsp
garlic clove	1, crushed
or garlic purée (paste)	5 ml/1 tsp
cumin seeds	10 ml/2 tsp
garam masala	10 ml/2 tsp
ground turmeric	5 ml/1 tsp
creamed coconut, roughly chopped	150 g/5 oz
tomato purée (paste)	15 ml/1 tbsp
very hot (not boiling) vegetable stock or water	600 ml/1 pint/2½ cups
fresh lime or lemon juice	15 ml/1 tbsp
salt and freshly ground black pepper	
aubergine (eggplant)	1, trimmed and diced
red (bell) pepper	1, seeded and cut into 2.5 cm/1 in pieces
carrot	1, sliced
large potato	1, peeled and diced
broccoli, cut into florets	200 g/7 oz
frozen peas	100 g/4 oz/⅔ cup, thawed
bay leaf	1

1 Heat the ghee or butter in a large saucepan, add the onion and fry for 6–7 minutes, until it is almost soft. Add the garlic, cumin seeds, garam masala and turmeric and cook for a further minute, stirring all the time.

2 Add the coconut, tomato purée and about half of the stock or water, and stir until the coconut has melted. Turn off the heat, stir in the citrus juice and season with salt and pepper.

3 Put the aubergine, red pepper, carrot, potato, broccoli and peas in the ceramic cooking pot. Add the bay leaf. Pour over the spicy coconut sauce. Cover with the lid, switch the slow cooker to High and cook for 3 hours or to Low for 6 hours, or until the vegetables are tender.

4 Remove the bay leaf, taste the curry and adjust the seasoning if necessary.

5 Serve with basmati rice or spiced naan breads.

variations

- You can ring the changes with different vegetables such as courgettes (zucchini) instead of aubergines (eggplants) or cauliflower instead of broccoli.

chick pea curry

Pomegranate molasses – a dark sticky reduction of pomegranate juices – adds a sweet and tart flavour and rich colour.

SERVES 4
READY IN 3–4 HOURS ON LOW   ②

groundnut (peanut) or sunflower oil	30 ml/2 tbsp
large onion,	1, chopped
or frozen diced onion	60 ml/2 tbsp
grated fresh or bottled ginger	15 ml/1 tbsp
ground turmeric	5 ml/1 tsp
chilli powder	2.5 ml/½ tsp
garam masala	2.5 ml/½ tsp
hot (not boiling) vegetable stock	150 ml/¼ pint/⅔ cup
tomato purée (paste)	10 ml/2 tsp
ripe tomatoes	350 g/12 oz, skinned, seeded and chopped
can of chick peas (garbanzos)	400 g/14 oz/large, drained and rinsed
pomegranate molasses	15 ml/1 tbsp
salt and freshly ground black pepper	

1 Heat the oil in a frying pan. Add the onion and cook for 7–8 minutes until soft. Stir in the ginger, ground turmeric, chilli powder and garam masala and cook for a further 30 seconds. Turn off the heat and stir in the stock and tomato purée.

2 Tip the mixture into the ceramic cooking pot, then stir in the tomatoes, chick peas and pomegranate molasses. Season with salt and pepper.

3 Cover with the lid and cook on Low for 3–4 hours or until the tomatoes are very pulpy and the sauce is thick. Taste and adjust the seasoning if necessary.

4 Serve with warmed naan bread or parathas.

tip

- You can buy pomegranate molasses in ethnic stores or large supermarkets.

aubergine and lentil madras

This makes a great vegetarian meal or you can serve as an accompaniment to a chicken or lamb curry, or with grilled poultry or meat.

SERVES 4
READY IN **4½ HOURS ON LOW**   ③

red split lentils	175 g/6 oz/1 cup
very hot (not boiling) vegetable stock or water	750 ml/1½ pints/3 cups
large waxy potatoes	2, peeled and cut into 2.5 cm/1 in chunks
large aubergine (eggplant)	1, trimmed and cut into 2.5 cm/1 in chunks
can of fried onions in olive oil	400 g/14 oz/large
garlic clove	1, crushed
or garlic purée (paste)	5 ml/1 tsp
Madras curry paste	45 ml/3 tbsp
thick plain yoghurt	150 ml/¼ pint/⅔ cup
frozen peas	100 g/4 oz/⅔ cup
salt	to taste

1 Rinse the lentils in a sieve (strainer) under cold running water, then tip them into the ceramic cooking pot with the stock or water. Switch on the slow cooker to High and leave to cook for a few minutes while preparing the rest of the ingredients.

2 Add the potatoes, aubergine and onions to the slow cooker. In a bowl, stir the garlic and curry paste with a little of the yoghurt to blend, then stir in the rest of the yoghurt. Pour over the vegetables and lentils and stir everything together.

3 Cover with the lid and cook on High for a further 2 hours or on Low for 4 hours or until the lentils, potatoes and aubergine are tender.

4 Meanwhile, allow the peas to thaw in the sieve. Briefly rinse with boiling water, then stir into the curry. Cook for a further 15 minutes on High or 30 minutes on Low.

5 Taste and season with salt before serving with warmed naan bread.

tip

- Always buy good-quality curry pastes for the best flavour.

eggs in mughlai sauce

Mughlai cuisine dates back to the 16th century, yet is still popular today. Its dishes are characterised by aromatic sauces.

SERVES 4
READY IN **2¼-4¼ HOURS ON LOW** ②

groundnut (peanut) or sunflower oil	15ml/1 tbsp
onion,	1, chopped
or frozen diced onion	45 ml/3 tbsp
grated fresh or bottled ginger	15 ml/1 tbsp
cayenne pepper	1.5 ml/¼ tsp
ground cumin	5 ml/1 tsp
ground coriander	5 ml/1 tsp
garam masala	2.5 ml/½ tsp
salt	2.5 ml/½ tsp
lemon juice	15 ml/1 tbsp
tomato purée (paste)	10 ml/2 tsp
vegetable stock	120 ml/4 fl oz/½ cup
cornflour (cornstarch)	5 ml/1 tsp
single (light) cream	250 ml/8 fl oz/1 cup
eggs	6–8, at room temperature
chopped fresh or thawed frozen coriander (cilantro)	30 ml/2 tbsp

1 Heat the oil in a frying pan, add the onion and cook for 10 minutes, stirring from time to time until it just begins to colour. Stir in the ginger, cayenne pepper, cumin, ground coriander and garam masala and cook for a further minute. Turn off the heat.

2 Stir in the salt, lemon juice, tomato purée and vegetable stock. Tip the mixture into the ceramic cooking pot, scraping the pan well.

3 Blend the cornflour with a little of the cream in a bowl, then stir in the rest of the cream. Add to the spice mixture in the pot and mix well. Cover with the lid and switch the slow cooker on to Low. Cook the sauce for 2–4 hours.

4 About 20 minutes before you are ready to serve, bring a pan of water to the boil, lower in the eggs one at a time, then hard-boil for 7–8 minutes (depending on whether the eggs are medium-sized or large).

5 Plunge the eggs into cold water and leave for 2–3 minutes or until just cool enough to peel. Cut each egg in half lengthwise. Add the eggs to the sauce, replace the cover on the pot and cook for a further 15 minutes, until heated through.

6 Sprinkle with chopped coriander and serve with warmed Indian breads.

variation

- Instead of hard-boiled eggs, you could add ready-cooked vegetables or, for non-vegetarians, chicken, to the sauce and reheat until piping hot.

cauliflower and coconut dhal

Always use full-fat coconut milk when cooking in the slow cooker as half-fat versions may separate during cooking.

SERVES 4
READY IN 4¼–5¼ HOURS ON LOW

groundnut (peanut) or sunflower oil	15ml/1 tbsp
onion,	1, finely chopped
or frozen diced onion	45 ml/3 tbsp
garlic clove,	1, crushed
or garlic purée (paste)	5 ml/1 tsp
grated fresh or bottled ginger	10 ml/2 tsp
hot curry paste	45 ml/3 tbsp
red lentils	75 g/3 oz, washed and drained
very hot (not boiling) vegetable stock	250 ml/8 fl oz/1 cup
small cauliflower	1, cut into florets
can of coconut milk	400 ml/14 fl oz/large
salt and freshly ground black pepper	
frozen peas	100 g/4 oz/¾ cup, thawed
chopped fresh or frozen coriander (cilantro) or parsley	45 ml/2 tbsp
fresh or bottled lemon juice	15 ml/1 tbsp

1 Heat the oil in a frying pan and cook the onion for 6–7 minutes until almost soft. Add the garlic, ginger and curry paste and cook for 1 minute, stirring all the time. Turn off the heat and stir in the lentils and stock.

2 Put the cauliflower in the ceramic cooking pot. Pour in the spicy onion mixture and stir to coat, then add the coconut milk. Season with salt and pepper, then stir again.

3 Cover with the lid and cook on Low for 4–5 hours or until the cauliflower is tender and the lentils have cooked to a pulpy sauce. Stir in the peas and cook for a further 15 minutes.

4 Stir in the coriander or parsley and lemon juice, then taste and adjust the seasoning if necessary.

5 Serve with naan bread.

tip

- If canned coconut milk is unavailable, use 150 g/5 oz creamed coconut mixed with 400 ml/14 fl oz/1¾ cups boiling water.

indian potatoes and okra

Also known as ladies' fingers or bhindi, okra is used extensively in Indian cooking and its sticky juices help thicken and enrich dishes.

SERVES 4
READY IN 4–6 HOURS ON LOW ②

large onion	1, roughly chopped
or frozen diced onion	60 ml/4 tbsp
garlic cloves,	2, peeled
or garlic purée (paste)	10 ml/2 tsp
grated fresh or bottled ginger	30 ml/2 tbsp
groundnut (peanut) or sunflower oil	30 ml/2 tbsp
red chilli,	1, seeded and finely chopped
or chilli purée (paste)	5 ml/1 tsp
black mustard seeds	5 ml/1 tsp
ground coriander	5 ml/1 tsp
ground cumin	5 ml/1 tsp
ground turmeric	2.5 ml/½ tsp
very hot (not boiling) vegetable stock	400 ml/14 fl oz/1¾ cups
can of chopped tomatoes	400 g/14 oz/large
okra	175 g/6 oz, trimmed and sliced
potatoes	450 g/1 lb, peeled and cut into large chunks
sultanas (golden raisins)	25 g/1 oz
salt and freshly ground black pepper	

1 Put the onion, garlic and ginger in a food processor and blend to a smooth purée (paste). Heat the oil in a large saucepan and pour in the purée and add the chilli. Cook over a low heat for 5 minutes, stirring frequently.

2 Add the mustard seeds, ground coriander, cumin and turmeric and cook for a further minute. Turn off the heat. Pour in roughly a third of the stock and stir well. Tip into the ceramic cooking pot.

3 Add the chopped tomatoes, okra, potatoes and sultanas to the pot. Season with salt and pepper. Pour in the rest of the stock and mix well. Cover with the lid and switch the slow cooker on to Low.

4 Cook for 4–6 hours or until the vegetables are tender. If having as a main dish, top with a spoonful of plain yoghurt.

5 Serve with rice or Indian breads.

tip

- Always use chillis or chilli purée to suit your own taste.

paneer korma

Unlike most cheese, paneer does not contain rennet, so is suitable for vegetarians. It is now sold in most supermarkets.

SERVES 4
READY IN 5 HOURS ON LOW

shallots,	4, finely chopped
or frozen chopped shallots	45 ml/3 tbsp
garlic clove,	1, crushed
or garlic purée (paste)	5 ml/1 tsp
red chilli,	1, seeded and finely chopped
or red chilli purée (paste)	5 ml/1 tsp
ground coriander	5 ml/1 tsp
ground cumin	5 ml/1 tsp
ground turmeric	5 ml/1 tsp
garam masala	5 ml/1 tsp
can of chopped tomatoes	200 g/7 oz/small
tomato purée (paste)	15 ml/1 tbsp
soft light brown sugar	2.5 ml/½ tsp
boiling vegetable stock or water	150 ml/¼ pint/⅔ cup
salt and freshly ground black pepper	
frozen peas, thawed	175 g/6 oz/1 cup
single (light) cream	150 ml/¼ pint/⅔ cup
paneer	350 g/12 oz, cut into 2.5 cm/1 in cubes

Or for home-made paneer:
whole milk	1.75 litres/3 pints/7½ cups
lemon juice	20 ml/4 tsp

1 Put the shallots, garlic, chilli, ground coriander, cumin and turmeric, garam masala and chopped tomatoes into the ceramic cooking pot.

2 Stir the tomato purée and sugar into the boiling stock or water and carefully pour into the pot. Season with salt and pepper, stir, then cover with the lid and cook on High for 2 hours or on Low for 4 hours, or until the shallots are very tender.

3 Put the peas in a sieve (strainer) and briefly rinse with boiling water (so that they will quickly heat when added to the cooking pot). Add to the pot with the cream. Stir well, then add the paneer and gently mix everything together. Replace the lid and cook for a further 30 minutes on High or 1 hour on Low, or until the paneer is heated through and the peas are cooked.

4 Taste and adjust the seasoning if necessary and serve with popadoms or Indian Potatoes and Okra (page 134).

to make the paneer:

1 Gently warm the milk over a medium heat. When it starts to boil, add the lemon juice and stir well. After 5–7 minutes, the milk will separate into curds (white lumps) and whey (thin yellow liquid).

2 Turn off the heat and drain through a sieve lined with muslin (cheesecloth). Discard the whey, or use it in baking.

3 Tie up the cloth and place it in the sieve over a bowl. Put a weight on top, a plate with a can of beans on top for example, then leave in the fridge to drip and compress for at least 6 hours, or overnight, until the cheese is firm. Use within four days.

vegetables with jaipuri spices

Jaipur, also known as 'the pink city' is the capital of the Indian state of Rajasthan. Food from this region tends to be mild.

SERVES 4
READY IN **5½ HOURS ON LOW**   ①

groundnut (peanut) or sunflower oil	30 ml/2 tbsp
cumin seeds	5 ml/1 tsp
large onion,	1, chopped
or frozen diced onion	60 ml/2 tbsp
rogan josh curry paste	30 ml/2 tbsp
very hot (not boiling) vegetable stock or water	250 ml/8 fl oz/1 cup
large potato	1, about 225 g/8 oz, peeled and diced
large carrots	2, peeled, halved lengthways and sliced
green beans	225 g/8 oz, trimmed and halved
tomatoes	4, skinned and seeded, if preferred, chopped
frozen peas	175 g/6 oz
fresh or bottled lemon juice	15 ml/1 tbsp
salt and freshly ground black pepper	
thick plain or Greek-style yoghurt	45 ml/3 tbsp
chopped fresh or frozen coriander (cilantro)	30 ml/2 tbsp
flaked (slivered) toasted almonds	50 g/2 oz/½ cup

1 Heat the oil in a frying pan, then add the cumin seeds. When they smell fragrant, stir in the onion. Cook for 6–7 minutes until starting to colour. Stir in the curry paste and cook for a further 30 seconds. Turn off the heat.

2 Gradually add the stock or water to the pan, stirring to mix. Put the potato, carrots, green beans and tomatoes into the ceramic cooking pot and pour over the spicy onion mixture.

3 Cover with the lid and cook on High for 2½ hours or on Low for 5 hours, until the vegetables are tender.

4 Meanwhile, let the peas thaw in a sieve (strainer). Pour over some boiling water to heat them and add to the cooking pot with the lemon juice. Season with salt and pepper. Stir, then replace the lid and cook for a further 15 minutes on High, 30 minutes on Low.

5 Stir in the yoghurt and most of the chopped coriander. Taste and adjust the seasoning if necessary. Sprinkle with the remaining coriander and flaked almonds.

6 Serve hot with Indian breads.

tip
- Use full-fat plain or Greek-style yoghurt, or the sauce may split and separate.

vegetable vindaloo

Originally brought to Goa by the Portuguese (the 'vin' part refers to the wine or vinegar in the dish), this curry is fiery.

SERVES 4
READY IN **4¾ HOURS ON LOW**   ③

vindaloo curry paste	45 ml/3 tbsp
lemon juice	15 ml/1 tbsp
soft brown sugar	5 ml/1 tsp
hot vegetable stock	150 ml/¼ pint/⅔ cup
cauliflower florets	350g/12 oz (about half a head)
courgettes (zucchini)	3, thickly sliced
chick peas (garbanzos)	400 g/14 oz/large can, rinsed
passata (sieved tomatoes)	350 ml/12 fl oz/1⅓ cups
baby spinach leaves	150 g/5 oz
salt	to taste

1 Put the curry paste, lemon juice and sugar in the pot. Blend in a few spoonfuls of the stock, then stir in the rest of the stock. Add the cauliflower, courgettes, chick peas and passata.

2 Cover with the lid and cook on High for 2 hours or on Low for 4 hours until the cauliflower is tender.

3 Place the spinach on top of the vegetables, pushing it down into the hot liquid. Replace the lid and cook for a further 30–45 minutes or until wilted.

4 Stir the spinach into the vegetable mixture. Season with salt to taste.

5 Serve with basmati rice, popadoms and Cucumber and Coriander Raita (page 158).

side dishes and accompaniments

It's the side dishes and accompaniments that turn an Indian curry into a special occasion. No curry would be complete without a bowl of steaming basmati rice, either plain, pilau or one of the many flavoured variations suggested here. Many are best cooked conventionally to complement your slow-cooked curry. Mix and match as you like to create the perfect Indian meal.

The following side dishes can either be cooked conventionally on the hob, or in the slow cooker if you have cooked your curry the day before or if you are lucky enough to have two slow cookers.

In this chapter you'll also discover recipes for vegetable side dishes such as mushroom bhaji and Bombay potatoes, lentil dhals and accompaniments, including mango chutney.

cooking rice

White basmati rice – whether plain or cooked with spices or flavourings such as coconut – is a classic accompaniment to Indian curries and is considered to be the finest variety of rice.

Mainly grown in northern India, in the foothills of the Himalayas and in the Punjab, Basmati rice has fine slender grains and a unique aromatic taste and texture – the word 'basmati' means 'the fragrant one'. It is also possible to buy brown basmati rice.

Ordinary long-grain rice and basmati rice do not cook well in the slow cooker as the two types require fast boiling, but 'easy-cook' (also known as 'parboiled' or 'converted') rice is very successful and this type is very popular in India where the technique of preparing it was created. In spite of its name, 'easy-cook' rice takes almost half as long again to cook as most long grain rices, but the grains always stay separate after cooking.

The whole grain rice is soaked in water and then steamed, and for white rice the bran is then removed. The parboiled rice grains are more yellow than those of normal rice, but this discolouration disappears during cooking. In this chapter, you'll find recipes for cooking rice on the hob – ideal when you are cooking a curry in your slow cooker – and also several for cooking rice in the slow cooker.

Boiling rice: This is the easiest way to cook rice. Some varieties need to be rinsed or soaked first, so check the instructions on the packet. To accompany a main meal, allow 75 g/3 oz/⅓ cup per person.

Pan-of-water method: Half-fill a large pan with boiling water and add a pinch of salt (you need roughly 1.2 litres/

2 pints/5 cups for every 200 g/7 oz/1 cup rice). Heat until the water boils rapidly, then add the rice and bring it back to the boil. Turn down the heat a little and cook the rice for as long as it says on the packet (usually 10–15 minutes). Test it by removing a few grains; they should be just tender. Drain through a large sieve (strainer) or fine-holed colander. If you've used ordinary long-grain or basmati (rather than easy-cook) and it looks a bit 'sticky', pour a kettle of boiling water over it, drain again and stir gently with a fork to fluff up the grains. Stir in a little butter or chopped fresh herbs if you like. To keep warm, either return the rice to the pan and cover or leave in the sieve and set it over the pan with a little boiling water in the bottom.

Absorption method: To cook rice in a measured amount of water (or stock, which gives it a wonderful flavour), measure the rice in a cup, then add exactly double that amount of water (plus a little salt, to taste) or stock. Heat them both in the pan to boiling point, stir once, then turn down the heat a little. Cover the pan with a tight-fitting lid. Cook the rice for as long as it says on the pack. If any liquid is left, continue cooking without the lid for another minute. This method is perfect if you want to add flavourings to the rice.

Saffron Rice: Follow the absorption method of cooking rice. Soak a generous pinch of saffron strands in 30 ml/2 tbsp hot water for a few minutes. Add to the water or stock.

Turmeric Rice: Follow the absorption method of cooking rice, adding 5 ml/1 tsp ground turmeric, to the water or stock.

Coconut Rice: Follow the absorption method, substituting coconut milk for up to a third of the water or stock.

Lemon-scented Rice: Follow either the pan-of-water or the absorption method, adding a large strip of lemon rind to the stock or water. After cooking, add 15 g/½ oz butter and 30 ml/2 tbsp fresh or bottled lemon juice to the rice and stir well. If serving with a dish that has a very rich and creamy sauce, leave out the butter.

mushroom pilau

Serve this on its own as a light lunch or supper dish or as an accompaniment to a meat or chicken curry.

SERVES 4
READY IN **1 HOUR ON LOW**
①

ghee or unsalted (sweet) butter or sunflower oil	30 ml/2 tbsp
shallots,	2, finely chopped
or frozen chopped shallots	30 ml/2 tbsp
garlic clove,	1, crushed
or garlic purée (paste)	5 ml/1 tsp
freshly grated or bottled ginger	10 ml/2 tsp
button mushrooms, sliced	175 g/6 oz/2½ cups
easy-cook (converted) basmati rice	250 g/9 oz/1⅓ cups
thinly pared strip of lemon rind (optional)	
garam masala	2.5 ml/½ tsp
very hot (not boiling) vegetable stock	500 ml/17 fl oz/2¼ cups
salt and freshly ground black pepper	
chopped fresh or frozen coriander (cilantro)	60 ml/4 tbsp

1 Heat the ghee, butter or oil in a large frying pan. Add the shallots and gently cook for 5 minutes, then stir in the garlic, ginger and mushrooms and cook for 2–3 minutes or until the mushrooms are beginning to colour and soften.

2 Stir in the rice, lemon rind, if using, and garam masala. Turn off the heat and tip the mixture into the ceramic cooking pot. Pour over the stock and season with salt and pepper. Mix everything together.

3 Cover with the lid and switch on the slow cooker to High. Cook for 50 minutes to 1 hour or until the rice is tender and has absorbed all the stock. Fluff up the rice with a fork, taste and adjust the seasoning, if necessary, and stir through the coriander before serving.

tip

- If you prefer a stronger mushroom flavour, use field or large open mushrooms and roughly chop them instead of slicing.

bombay potatoes

Traditionally these are made by parboiling then frying in oil. It's so much simpler and healthier to make them in the slow cooker.

SERVES 4
READ IN **6 HOURS ON LOW**   ②

ghee or unsalted (sweet) butter	15 ml/1 tbsp
groundnut (peanut) or sunflower oil	15ml/1 tbsp
green chilli,	1, seeded and finely chopped
or green chilli paste	5 ml/1 tsp
ground coriander	5 ml/1 tsp
ground cumin	5 ml/1 tsp
ground turmeric	2.5 ml/½ tsp
hot (but not boiling) vegetable stock or water	90 ml/6 tbsp
potatoes	700 g/1½ lb, peeled and cut into 4 cm/1½ in chunks
salt and freshly ground black pepper	

1 Heat the ghee or butter and oil together in a small frying pan. Add the chilli, ground coriander, cumin and turmeric and stir over a medium heat for 30 seconds. Turn off the heat and stir in the stock.

2 Put the potatoes in the ceramic cooking pot and season with salt and pepper. Pour over the spice mixture and stir well.

3 Cover with the lid and cook on High for 3 hours or on Low for 6 hours or until the potatoes are very tender.

4 Taste and adjust the seasoning if necessary. Stir in some diced tomatoes and chopped fresh or thawed frozen coriander, if you like, before serving.

tip

• If you like, you can stir in some skinned and diced tomato and chopped fresh coriander (cilantro) at the end of cooking.

mushroom bhaji

It's important to pre-fry the mushrooms to give them a good brown colour. Also lovely made with whole baby button mushrooms.

SERVES 4

READY IN 4 HOURS ON LOW

ghee or unsalted (sweet) butter	15 ml/1 tbsp
small onion,	1, chopped
or frozen diced onion	30 ml/2 tbsp
garlic cloves,	2, crushed
or garlic purée (paste)	10 ml/2 tsp
button mushrooms	350 g/12 oz, thickly sliced
ground coriander	5 ml/1 tsp
ground cumin	5 ml/1 tsp
ground turmeric	2.5 ml/½ tsp
chilli powder	2.5 ml/½ tsp
salt	1.5 ml/¼ tsp
tomato purée (paste)	10 ml/2 tsp
hot (not boiling) light vegetable stock or water	60 ml/4 tbsp
chopped fresh or frozen coriander (cilantro) or parsley	30 ml/2 tbsp

1 Melt the ghee or butter in a frying pan and cook the onion for 3–4 minutes. Add the garlic and mushrooms, turn up the heat a little and cook for 5 minutes, or until the mushrooms and onion are slightly browned.

2 Add the ground coriander, cumin, turmeric and chilli powder and cook for a further 30 seconds. Turn off the heat and stir in the salt, tomato purée and stock. Tip the mixture into the ceramic cooking pot.

3 Cover with the lid and cook on High for 2 hours or Low for 4 hours or until the mushrooms and onions are very tender.

4 Stir in the chopped coriander or parsley. Taste and adjust the seasoning if necessary before serving.

tip

- The tomato purée helps to flavour and thicken the juices, but you can leave it out if you prefer.

makhani dhal

Traditionally dhal is cooked over a very low flame for several hours giving it a richer flavour and smooth texture.

SERVES 4
READY IN 5–6 HOURS ON LOW

dried split black lentils (urad dal)	225 g/8 oz/1⅓ cups
large onion,	1, finely chopped
or frozen diced onions	60 ml/4 tbsp
ghee or butter	30 ml/2 tbsp
garlic cloves,	2, peeled and crushed
or garlic purée (paste)	10 ml/2 tsp
green chillies,	2, seeded and finely chopped
or green chilli purée	10 ml/2 tsp
grated fresh or bottled ginger	15 ml/1 tbsp
ground coriander	10 ml/2 tsp
ground cumin	10 ml/2 tsp
ground turmeric	5 ml/1 tsp
chilli powder	2.5 ml/½ tsp
very hot (not boiling) vegetable stock	1.5 litres/2½ pints/6 cups
bay leaves	2
can red kidney beans	400 g/14 oz/large, drained
tomatoes	2, quartered, seeded and chopped
double (heavy) cream	150 ml/¼ pint/⅔ cup
garam masala	2.5 ml/½ tsp
chopped fresh or frozen coriander (cilantro)	60 ml/4 tbsp
salt and freshly ground black pepper	

1 Put the lentils in a bowl and cover with cold water. Leave to soak for a few minutes while preparing the rest of the ingredients. Cook the onion in the ghee or butter in a large frying pan for 6–7 minutes until almost soft.

2 Add the garlic, green chillies, ginger, ground coriander, cumin, turmeric and chilli powder. Cook for 1 more minute, stirring. Stir in about 150 ml/¼ pint/⅔ cup of the stock or water into the pan, then tip the mixture into the ceramic cooking pot. Add the bay leaves.

3 Rinse the lentils in a sieve (strainer) under cold running water and add to the pot. Pour in the rest of the stock or water, cover with the lid and cook on Low for 4–5 hours or until the lentils are tender.

4 Briefly rinse the kidney beans with boiling water to warm them and drain. Add to the cooking pot with the tomatoes, cream and garam masala. Replace the lid and cook for a further hour. Stir in the chopped coriander and season with salt and pepper to taste.

variations

- You can reduce the ghee or butter a little and use Greek-style yoghurt instead of cream for a healthier dish.

- For a vegan version, replace the butter with oil and the cream with thick coconut milk.

tip

- Dried split black lentils or urad dal are available from Indian food stores and some major supermarkets.

tarka dhal

Dhal is one of the staples of Indian cooking. It usually has a sauce-like consistency, but here it is a little thicker.

SERVES 4
READY IN 4 HOURS ON LOW ②

red split lentils	225 g/8 oz
ground turmeric	2.5 ml/½ tsp
grated fresh or bottled ginger	10 ml/2 tsp
green chilli,	1, seeded and finely chopped
or green chilli purée (paste)	5 ml/1 tsp
can of chopped tomatoes	200 g/7 oz/small
very hot (not boiling) vegetable stock or water	1 litre/1¾ pints/4¼ cups
chopped fresh or frozen coriander (cilantro)	60 ml/4 tbsp
salt and freshly ground black pepper	
For the tarka:	
groundnut (peanut) or sunflower oil	15ml/1 tbsp
cumin seeds	5 ml/1 tsp
black mustard seeds	10 ml/2 tsp
garlic cloves	2, finely sliced
dried red chillies	a pinch

1 Put the lentils in a bowl and cover with cold water. Leave to soak for a few minutes while preparing the rest of the ingredients. Rinse them under cold running water in a sieve (strainer), drain, then tip into the ceramic cooking pot.

2 Add the turmeric, ginger, chilli and tomatoes. Pour in the stock or water. Stir, then cover with the lid and cook on High for 2 hours or Low for 4 hours or until the lentils are very tender and have absorbed most of the liquid. If possible give the mixture a stir about half an hour before the end of cooking time to prevent it sticking.

3 Meanwhile, make the tarka. Heat the oil in a small frying pan and cook the cumin and mustard seeds for a few seconds. Add the garlic and dried chillies and fry, stirring constantly for 1–2 minutes or until the garlic is pale golden.

4 Stir the chopped coriander into the dhal and season with salt and pepper. Spoon into a warmed bowl and serve with the tarka drizzled over the top.

tip

- Use the tarka to spice up other lentil dishes.

potato and cauliflower curry

Popular in Northern India, 'gobi aloo' makes a great alternative to serve with meat dishes instead of rice.

SERVES 4

READY IN **6 HOURS ON LOW**

groundnut (peanut) or sunflower oil	30 ml/2 tbsp
large onion,	1, chopped
or frozen diced onion	60 ml/2 tbsp
garlic clove,	1, crushed
or garlic purée (paste)	5 ml/1 tsp
grated fresh or bottled ginger	5 ml/1 tsp
cumin seeds	5 ml/1 tsp
coriander seeds	2.5 ml/½ tsp
ground turmeric	5 ml/1 tsp
dried chilli flakes	a pinch
small cauliflower	1, cut into florets
large potatoes	2, peeled and cut into bite-sized chunks
very hot (not boiling) light vegetable stock or water	150 ml/¼ pint/⅔ cup
salt and freshly ground black pepper	

1 Heat the oil in a frying pan and cook the onion for 7–8 minutes, until almost soft. Stir in the garlic, ginger, cumin and coriander seeds, turmeric and chilli flakes. Fry, stirring continuously for 2 minutes.

2 Add the cauliflower and potatoes and stir until coated in the mixture. Stir in the stock or water and seasoning to taste.

3 Tip into the ceramic cooking pot, cover with the lid and cook on High for 3 hours or on Low for 6 hours, or until the vegetables are tender.

4 Stir gently, then taste and adjust the seasoning if necessary before serving.

tip

- Add a couple of skinned, seeded and chopped tomatoes with the vegetables for added colour and flavour.

sweet mango chutney

No Indian meal would be complete without this classic chutney. In restaurants it is often served as a dip with crisp popadoms.

MAKES 450 G/1 LB

READY IN **6 HOURS ON LOW + 1 ON HIGH**   ①

firm mangoes (slightly under-ripe ones are fine)	4
cider or white wine vinegar	120 ml/4 fl oz/½ cup
caster (superfine) sugar	200 g/7 oz/scant cup
garlic clove,	1, crushed
or garlic purée (paste)	5 ml/1 tsp
grated fresh or bottled ginger	30 ml/2 tbsp
crushed dried red chillies	1.5 ml/¼ tsp
bay leaves	2
salt	2.5 ml/½ tsp

1 Peel the mangoes and remove the stones, then roughly cut the flesh into small chunks. Put in the ceramic cooking pot with the vinegar. Stir, then cover with the lid and cook on High for 1½ hours or on Low for 3 hours, stirring the mixture halfway through cooking time.

2 Add the sugar, garlic, ginger, chillies, bay leaves and salt and stir until the sugar has dissolved. Replace the lid and cook for a further 1½ hours on High or 3 hours on Low.

3 Take off the lid and cook on High for a further 1 hour, stirring every 20 minutes or so, or until the chutney is reduced to a thick consistency.

4 Remove the bay leaves and spoon the hot chutney into warmed, sterilised jars and seal immediately.

5 When cold, store the jars in a cool, dark place and leave the chutney to mature for at least 2 weeks before eating. Use within 1 year. Once opened, keep it refrigerated.

tip

- For a hotter version, double the dried red chillies or add 2 finely chopped green chillies instead.

cucumber and coriander raita

Sprinkling the cucumber with salt draws out some of the moisture that would otherwise dilute the yoghurt.

SERVES 4
READY IN **20 MINS**
①

cucumber	½, grated
chopped fresh or frozen coriander (cilantro)	45 ml/3 tbsp
salt	1.5 ml/¼ tsp
thick plain or Greek-style yoghurt	300 ml/½ pint/1¼ cups

1 Put the cucumber in a stainless steel or plastic sieve (strainer) and sprinkle with the salt. Leave to drain for 15 minutes, then press out some of the juices with a back of a spoon.

2 Tip the cucumber into a bowl and stir in the yoghurt and coriander. Cover and chill in the fridge until needed. Garnish with a sprig of fresh coriander before serving, if you like.

index